Tibetan Buddhism & Modern Physics

A Quantum Mechanical Challenge Toward A Union of Love and Knowledge

VIC MANSFIELD

with a foreword by

HIS HOLINESS THE DALAI LAMA

New Age Books

Tibetan Buddhism & Modern Physics

ISBN: 978-81-7822-376-6

First Indian Edition: Delhi, 2011

First Edition Published by Templeton Foundation Press, 2008

Library of Congress Cataloging-in-Publication Data

Mansfield, Victor, 1941-
Tibetan Buddhism and Modern Physics:
A Quantum Mechanical Challenge/Vic Mansfield.
p.cm.
Includes bibliographical references and index.
ISBN: 978-81-7822-376-6 (pbk. : alk. paper)
1. Physics–Religious aspects–Buddhism. 2. Quantum theory–Religious aspects–Buddhism. 3. Buddhism and science. 4. Buddhism–China–Tibet–Doctrines. I. Title
BQ4570.P45M36 2008 294.3'3653—dc22

Published by
NEW AGE BOOKS
A-44, Naraina Industrial Area, Phase-I
New Delhi (India)-110 028
Email: nab@vsnl.in
Website: www.newagebooksindia.com

For Sale in Asia Only

Printed in India
at Shri Jainendra Press
A-45 Naraina Indl. Area, Phase-I, New Delhi-110 028

Tibetan Buddhism
&
Modern Physics

It clearly and engagingly addresses the complex issues of dialogue and collaboration between Buddhism and science, revealing connections and differences between the two. It strongly responds to the Dalai Lama's "heartfelt plea" for genuine collaboration between science and Buddhism.

Contents

Foreword

I HAVE A DEEP INTEREST in the close relationship between modern science and the study of the inner dimensions of the human mind. This is because we live in a physical world. We have a physical body and a mind, the two of which are closely interconnected. In fact, it is our experience of physical sensations and emotional responses as a consequence of these circumstances that make us sentient beings. Yet, if we compare the physical and mental influences upon our lives, it is clear that physical pain can be subdued by strength of mind; therefore, mental happiness and satisfaction are ultimately more important to us than physical discomfort and unhappiness. This is one of the reasons that spirituality, attention to our inner dimension, is so important. On the other hand, if someone is mentally unhappy, simple physical comfort does not relieve his or her mental distress.

I believe that it is the basic right of all beings, but particularly human beings, to lead a happy and successful life. In this context, science and technology have brought us a great deal of benefit. Because of advances in science and technology, some fundamental human problems have been solved, while other kinds of basic human misery, including disease and hunger, are being addressed. I have no doubt that science and technology can contribute toward the happiness of us all and that science is a vast and wonderful source of knowledge.

However, despite their achievements in many fields, we have not yet found a way to use science and technology to eliminate the worries and unhappiness that trouble so many people. Indeed, I think that the basic remedy for mental trouble, by nature, lies within the mind itself and that the potential for really solving problems of the mind exists only on a mental level. Therefore, while we certainly need science and technology, we also need a sense of spirituality, including ways to cultivate the warmheartedness and compassion that underpin our basic happiness.

Until recently, these two fields, science and spirituality, have remained distant and apart from each other, but I believe this is changing. For example, although I am a Buddhist, if I were to cling only to Buddhist teaching and deny what modern scientific findings prove, I would believe that the world is flat and at the center of the universe and that the sun and the moon revolve around it. Clearly, if I were to adopt an extreme stance and only consider what the scriptures say, keeping my distance from science, then I myself would suffer, not least due to a lack of knowledge.

The Buddhist tradition, particularly the thousand-year-old tradition of the Indian University of Nalanda that we inherited in Tibet, is concerned with trying to know reality, various levels of reality, through investigation, avoiding the pitfalls of underestimation and exaggeration. Modern science, too, is concerned with discovering reality, not only in theory but also in practice by conducting repeatable experiments. Whether we approach reality through science or through a spiritual path, we have to accept it as it is.

Vic Mansfield, whom I have known for many years, is someone who has reconciled his professional involvement with science with a deep interest in spirituality, and Tibetan Buddhism, in particular. He has taught and written widely about both. In this book, he has set out specifically to show how religion and spirituality are compatible with life in the modern world. I am grateful to him for responding to my appeal to people who have such knowledge to share it with others.

In today's world, we no longer live in the kind of isolation that allows us to dismiss views that are different from our own, for to do so can only be a source of conflict. Our increasing interdependence requires that we try to understand and appreciate other points of view. Readers will surely be rewarded by the light this book shines on the corresponding, but quite different, approaches to reality taken by Tibetan Buddhism and modern physics.

The Dalai Lama
November 23, 2007

Acknowledgments

Over three decades of teaching have taught me that instruction is most effective when the teacher is motivated by love for the students and the subject matter. With these twin loves present and reinforcing each other, teaching truly quickens the mind and brings life out of darkness. I have been enormously fortunate in receiving much inspired teaching, and I therefore organize my acknowledgements by thanking my many teachers for their loving instruction. Although not all of them are still alive, their benign influence still lives in me.

I give thanks to the Sisters of Mercy, brides of Christ, who provided my first opening to the inner world and helped me express my religious urge. Moving to the Norwalk, Connecticut, public-school system in ninth grade was a major awakening. There I felt the radiant affirmation of Mrs. Fitzgerald, my homeroom teacher. I am deeply grateful for her gift of life-saving water to a thirsty plant. I give special thanks to Mrs. Donovan for revealing the startling beauty and depth of Shakespeare. I thank Mr. Gilmore for showing me the joy of mathematics and the rigorous of thought it afforded. I give special thank to Mr. Maruca, my woodworking shop instructor. He taught kindness by his every action.

I am also grateful for Mr. Gilmore's teaching of high school chemistry. As explained in my second book, *Head and Heart: A Personal Exploration of Science and the Sacred,* without Mr. Gilmore's love and inspiration, I would never have become a scientist. I am thankful that I have had the privilege of telling this directly to him in a public lecture. I offer gratitude to Mr. Clark for instruction in advanced algebra and analytic geometry—a virtuoso dance between kindness and mathematical rigor. Then I did not appreciate how little our culture values such people. I now more fully realize how the twin loves of their students and their subject matter sustained their dedication and nourished me.

My horizons expanded enormously at Dartmouth College, where a diverse array of extraordinary teachers fired my love of science and the liberal arts. I thank Professor Sears for awakening me to the joyous exploration of the natural world through physics. I offer special thanks to Professor Doyle for showing me the extraordinary beauty of Maxwell's equations of electromagnetism. Without his inspired teaching, physics would have never made me its student. I offer special gratitude to Professor Christy who plunged me into the beauty and mystery of quantum mechanics, a subject that has held me captive for four decades. I thank Professor Laspere for his teaching excellence and unstinting support as my master's thesis advisor. My sincere gratitude extends to several members of the philosophy department of Dartmouth, not all of whose names I can recall after more than four decades. They team-taught an introduction to Western philosophy that opened my eyes to the wonder, rigor, and delight of philosophic thought.

At Cornell University special thank go to Professor Mermin. He elevated physics teaching to a high art form and deepened my understanding of quantum mechanics. I offer special thanks to Professor Terzian whose faith in me and unbounded enthusiasm for science sustained me during years of intense doubt. Special gratitude goes to Professor Spitzer who taught me how gentleness and intellectual rigor can combine into an inspiring year of graduate mathematics. I thank Professor Gottfried whose brilliant teaching threw a penetrating light into the depths of the quantum world. I express deep gratitude to Professor Salpeter, a man of extraordinary kindness and scientific brilliance, for drawing the best out of me as my research mentor.

Moving westward, I thank Professor Petrosian of Stanford University. When my spiritual journey called me to California for extended explorations of the murky depths of the psyche, he kept my interest in physics alive. Without doubt, his unique combination of generosity and scientific excellence allowed me to return to Cornell and complete my Ph.D.

I end my academic homage by offering special thanks to Colgate University, which has been my home for most of the last three decades. I never cease to be amazed at what a privilege it is to be a professor. I have especially appreciated the opportunities to teach in the General Education Program, where my Tibet course found a happy home. In particular,

I thank the members of the Physics and Astronomy Department, who have supported my unconventional interests. Each of my departmental colleagues has been my teacher in many ways, but I especially thank Professors Galvez and Malin for helping me appreciate various wonders of the natural world. Finally, I thank Peter Tagtmeyer, research librarian extraordinaire. Through hard work and wizardry, he repeatedly found the smallest needles in the largest haystacks.

Outside of academia, friends have showered much love on me over the decades. I especially thank my many brothers and sisters at Wisdom's Goldenrod Center for Philosophic Studies. They have shared with me nearly four decades of interest in spiritual, philosophic, and religious study and their associated meditation disciplines. Although too numerous to mention all of them, I especially thank Avery Solomon, Richard Goldman, Lauren Cottrell, and Andrew Holmes. I offer singular thanks to my good friend and editor Paul Cash, who directly showed his affection by making many helpful suggestions for improvements to this book.

Beyond Goldenrod, I particularly wish to thank Craig Preston and Lharampa Geshe Thupten Kunkhen for their patience, generosity, and sharing of their understanding of many subtle points within Tibetan Buddhism. I offer heartfelt thanks to Dr. Alan Wallace and Dr. Jordi Pigem for extensive and helpful comments on an early draft of this book.

I offer sincere thanks to the Templeton Foundation Press for the care lavished on this book and me. Their idealism and commitment to excellence is truly inspiring. I particularly thank Laura Barrett, acquisitions/managing editor, and the editor Mary Lou Bertucci for their dedication and skill at every step in the publishing process.

I conclude by turning to the immense love showered upon me by spiritual teachers. I offer them my deepest appreciation, fully aware that words cannot convey the burden of my heart. I first offer deep gratitude to my wife and best friend Elaine. She has helped me through innumerable intellectual and emotional thickets for nearly four decades. I thank her most of all for teaching me about the depth and sublime beauty of love. I offer deepest gratitude to my root guru Anthony Damiani. Although he has been dead for nearly a quarter of a century, he vividly lives in my heart, where I offer him thanks every day for sharing his passionate and penetrating analysis of several great religious traditions, both East and West. He taught me how to meditate and the supreme importance of attempting a personal realization of the great truths embodied in these noble traditions.

I give thanks to the late Paul Brunton for his encyclopedic writings and personal example of Himalayan spiritual heights. I especially thank him for encouraging me to write about science and spirituality. I offer special gratitude to the late Shri Shankara of Konchipuram, India, the sixty-eighth holder of a title stretching back to the great Adi Shankara, the founder of Advaita Vedanta, the crown jewel of Hinduism. Although we spoke few words, I offer him my sincerest thanks for radiating his astonishing love and wisdom out of a great well of silence. I thank Father Raimon Panikkar whose knowledge and love showed me the true universality embodied in Catholicism. I especially thank him for encouraging me in my writing about science and spirituality. Finally, I offer profound thanks to His Holiness the Dalai Lama, a living expression of wisdom and compassion. Along with all he has taught me about Buddhism, his tireless efforts to understand the relationship between science and spirituality are a continuous inspiration for me. He has taught me that the collaboration between science and spirituality can be a great avenue for the relief of human suffering.

Tibetan Buddhism & Modern Physics

1. What Are Buddhism and Science?

Why Is a Dialogue Needed?

Introduction

It is the fall of 1979, the beginning of one of the greatest educational events in my life. His Holiness the Dalai Lama is getting off a light airplane at the Ithaca, New York, airport. We members of Wisdom's Goldenrod Center for Philosophic Studies are eagerly awaiting his arrival and deeply honored that he is visiting us during his first tour of North America. Although my knowledge of him is limited, I have high spiritual expectations. I am, therefore, surprised that the first thing he does in getting out of the little plane is to lay his hands on the aileron (the hinged flap on the trailing edge of an aircraft wing, used for controlling flight) and work it up and down. Being a physicist, I am delighted to see him examining the mechanics of flight.

Over the next few days, I am awed by the Dalai Lama's keen intelligence, his deep spirituality, and the force of his personality. The picture here shows him at that time with our teacher Anthony Damiani, the founder of Goldenrod. From their first meeting in 1979, the Dalai Lama and Anthony formed a deep friendship. Our group consequently has enjoyed a special relationship with His Holiness, and we have met with him several times through the ensuing years.

I soon learned that the Dalai Lama's interest in the aileron and the mechanics of flight expressed his lifelong interest in science and things mechanical, from the physical and life sciences to his interest in fixing watches. Although not formally trained in science, the Dalai Lama has a keen scientific aptitude. The internationally famous Austrian physicist Anton Zeilinger has spent many days discussing quantum physics with him—both in India and in Austria. A few years ago, Anton told me that he half jokingly invited the Dalai Lama to be his graduate student in physics. Anton has written, "His Holiness might have become a great

FIGURE 1.1.
His Holiness the Dalai Lama and Anthony Damiani (from the family album)

FIGURE 1.2.
His Holiness the Dalai Lama in 1991

physicist in another world without his duties as spiritual and political leader of the Tibetan people."[1]

That meeting in 1979 fanned the fires of my already decade-long interest in Buddhism and turned me more toward its Tibetan expression. While continuing my teaching and research in physics, I have had the good fortune to receive instruction from His Holiness upon many occasions, in groups both large and small. In the context of this book, it is relevant to recount briefly a visit that His Holiness made to Goldenrod in 1991, several years after our teacher Anthony had died.

During that visit, I took the photograph of the Dalai Lama that appears here as figure 1.2. Toward the end of that meeting, as an expression of our appreciation for the generosity of His Holiness toward our group, someone asked, "What can we do for you?" The Dalai Lama responded by requesting that we further the science and spirituality dialogue—not just the connection between science and Buddhism, but science and diverse traditions of spirituality. Since I was one of only three scientists in the group, I felt a strong personal responsibility to help fulfill that request. This feeling grew even stronger in 2005 when His Holiness concluded his book *The Universe in a Single Atom*[2] (about the science and Buddhism collaboration) with the following words: "May each of us, as a member of the human family, respond to the moral obligation to make this collaboration possible. This is my heartfelt plea." When the Dalai Lama mentions "moral obligation" and speaks of his "heartfelt plea," I must listen. Two years before his initial request in 1991, I had been making some effort in that direction by writing papers and books that discuss the interplay of science and spirituality.[3] The present book, based almost entirely on new writing with a few refinements and expansions of some earlier writing, is a further attempt to honor His Holiness's request.

There are also larger intellectual and spiritual currents at play. For example, Buddhism has proved to be a particularly portable religion. It began approximately 2,500 years ago in what is now northern India and then spread widely throughout Asia. In each of its migrations, whether into Japan, Thailand, or Tibet, it interacted with the indigenous culture and took a unique form reflective of that culture. Thus, as Buddha *dharma* (the teachings of Buddhism) moves to the West, if it is truly to take root and thrive in Western soil, then it must take on Western cultural forms. One of the greatest Western cultural attainments is modern science. It is therefore obvious and natural that, for Buddha *dharma* to come fully to the West, it must somehow interact with this cultural dominant. The Buddhism and science dialogue is an important part of Buddhism's migration to the West.

More important than even Buddha *dharma*'s coming to the West, our actual survival on the planet requires a substantial and sustained dialogue between science and various spiritual traditions. Many of the great tragedies that rack our age, from conflicts between modernity and fundamentalists of all sorts to various ecological crises, can be traced, at least in part, to tensions between science and religion. The physicist and comparative religion professor Ravi Ravindra thinks it is the pressing problem for our generation. He writes:

> It is possible to hope that modern science and ancient spiritual traditions can be integrated in some higher synthesis. I would even say that such a task is the most important of all that can be undertaken by contemporary intellectuals, for on such a synthesis depends not only the global survival of man but also the creation of the right environment, right both physically and metaphysically, for future generations.[4]

The Dalai Lama's sustained interest in the science and Buddhism dialogue and collaboration directly expresses his agreement with Ravindra.

His Holiness's long-term engagement with science is especially inspiring these days when many religious people in the United States are at odds with science.

The Dalai Lama's interest not only produced *The Universe in a Single Atom* but also spawned other books on the relationship between Buddhism and science, especially through the Mind and Life Conferences. For example, from a recent conference with His Holiness has come *The New Physics and Cosmology: Dialogues with the Dalai Lama*, edited by Arthur Zajonc.[5] The Dalai Lama has encouraged parallel efforts independent of his direct participation. For example, he asked Alan Wallace to edit a book of essays on Buddhism and science, which resulted in *Buddhism and Science: Breaking New Ground.*[6] I was honored to contribute to that book, which includes connections between Buddhism and the cognitive sciences along with discussions of the physical sciences. A dialogue between a monk and a physicist flowered as *The Quantum and the Lotus: A Journey to the Frontiers Where Science and Buddhism Meet* by Matthieu Ricard and Trinh Xuan Thuan, a book I reviewed for the journal *Science and Theology.*[7] In the spring of 2006, *Buddhist Thought and Applied Psychological Research*, edited by Nauriyal, Drummond, and Lal was published.[8] I was also honored to contribute an essay to that book on the relationship between Tibetan Buddhism and the psychology of C. G. Jung.

I have been inspired by all these efforts, but my approach here is different. Although I assume the reader has no technical background in either Buddhism or physics, I have tried to go deeper than previous attempts. Rather than start at an advanced level, I gradually develop both the Buddhism and the physics in sufficient depth to probe the connections between them in more detail.

There are many extraordinary connections between the most important modern developments in physics and the deepest truths of Tibetan Buddhism. These profound connections allow for a deeper understanding of both Buddhism and physics and offer rich opportunities for collaboration. While maintaining scholarly rigor, I link these connections with the feelings and struggles of a beginner on the quest of buddhahood. In other words, I try to pay homage to both the head and the heart.

I do not, however, use physics to "prove" the truths of Buddhism. Since physical theories are intrinsically impermanent, it is a guarantee of obsolescence to bind Buddhism or any philosophic view too tightly to a physical theory. What happens when the physics inevitably changes? Do the foundations of Buddhism shudder at each scientific revolution? Nevertheless, science is the reigning worldview in modern culture, and thus it is natural to ask how a philosophic or religious view relates to this dominant view.

As the Dalai Lama shows in *The Universe in a Single Atom*, the connections between Buddhism and science go well beyond modern physics. However, here I restrict myself to discussing Buddhism's many deep links with modern physics. What I say about Buddhism usually applies to all expressions of Mahayana, but the deepest connections I make apply specifically to the Middle Way Consequence School of Tibetan Buddhism (Prasangika Madhyamika), what many consider the highest expression of Mahayana Buddhist thought. Of course, there are many other interpretations of Mahayana Buddhism; but, in the interest of both depth of treatment and sharpness of focus, I restrict myself to the Prasangika, as interpreted by the philosophically dominant Gelukpa sect within Tibetan Buddhism.

My goal in this book is to be true to both the Middle Way Consequence School of Buddhism, which I consistently abbreviate throughout this book as the "Middle Way," and to modern physics. Although the discussion here assumes no sophisticated background in either Buddhism or physics, it yields many surprises and counterintuitive conclusions. Some of them are truly breathtaking. As they say in the Middle Way, the world appears one way but truly exists in another. My hope is that the vistas opened will ignite wonder and encourage readers to go deeper, both in understanding the emerging views and in drawing out their moral implications.

I begin by briefly summarizing the approach to knowledge in both modern science and Buddhism. Only within a sense of the similarities and differences between them can we address how science and Buddhism might interact and what they could possibly gain from being in dialogue with each other. In the following chapters, I connect Buddhism to topics such as the indistinguishable nature of elementary particles, quantum nonlocality, the noncausal process at the heart of quantum mechanics, and the physics of time. These topics have remarkable and detailed connections to the Middle Way view of emptiness. I discuss emptiness in detail in later chapters. Now it is enough to say that emptiness implies that nothing independently or inherently exists. Positively stated, all things and persons exist only through their mutual interdependence. Perhaps most surprising, the connections between Buddhism and physics have moral implications. I will try to show how the view of nature in modern physics not only has precise and detailed connections to the Middle Way, but it also must issue in compassionate action, to a deeper concern for each other and our environment. Knowledge must issue in love, hence, the subtitle for this book.

Let us begin the exploration with a short foray into the early history of physics, where I focus on a seminal example of the intellectual curiosity expressed by the Dalai Lama's interest in the aileron.

Knowledge in Science and Buddhism

Let us take an imaginary trip to late sixteenth-century Pisa, Italy. There, Galileo Galilei, one of the greatest of the founding fathers of modern science, is just entering the ancient cathedral at Pisa. He is still a student at the University of Pisa and his scientific discoveries have not yet brought him into conflict with the Catholic Church. Soon the sermon begins, and the priest's voice echoes off the soaring vaults of the cathedral while the warm breeze gently rocks the great chandelier shown in the photo below. The arc length of the chandelier swing increases with the strength of the breeze. Galileo notices that the period, the time it takes to swing from its farthest position on one side all the way to the other side and back again, appears to be independent of its arc length (the distance it has to travel). To test this idea, he times the period using his pulse.

Knowing that mechanical clocks and the scientific method had not yet been developed, every scientist who hears of Galileo's early measurements on the swinging chandelier is amazed at his originality, ingenuity, and creativity. These preliminary measurements motivated Galileo to develop a clock based on the flow of water and initiated his long study of the pendulum. This study helped lay the foundation for the science of mechanics, the physics used to put an astronaut on the moon or to understand the motion of a ball in flight.

Let's take a closer look at the physics of the chandelier, or more precisely, the physics of the pendulum. Following Galileo, we reduce the pendulum to its essentials: a mass M on a weightless line of length L as shown in figure 1.4. You can closely approximate a simple pendulum by just hanging a stone of mass, M, from a string of length, L. Then, rather

FIGURE 1.3. *Galileo's chandelier (from Joseph Lupia)*

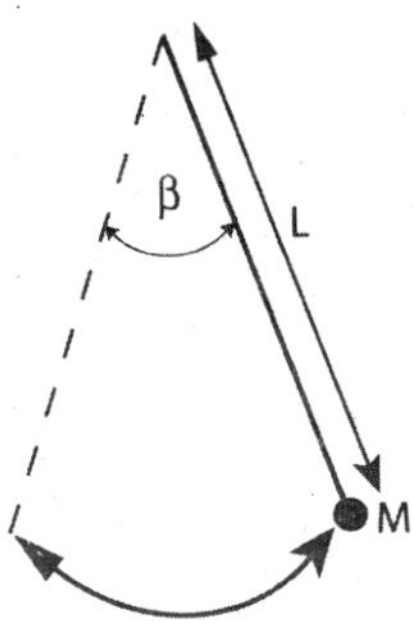

FIGURE 1.4. *(left) Simple pendulum*

than use your heartbeat, take a wristwatch or a simple kitchen timer and time its period, the time it takes to swing from one extreme to the other and back. We can make our experiment much more accurate if we time how long it takes the pendulum to swing for ten full periods and then divide this final time by ten.

With our timer and surprisingly little effort, we can find two important properties of the pendulum. First, as long as the angle corresponding to the arc (shown as β in the diagram) is small, say less then 20°, the period of the pendulum is independent of the arc length. In other words, a pendulum just barely swinging and one with a 20° arc would have the same period of oscillation. Here is an interesting and not obvious result. Second, we find that the period of the pendulum varies with the square root of *L*. For example, if we increase *L* by a factor of four the period becomes twice as long.

The detailed physics of the pendulum is not important for my present purposes, except as an illustration of the acquisition of knowledge in physics. With the pendulum in mind, I enumerate some critical presuppositions of physics for comparison and contrast with the relevant features of Buddhism. I start with features of science that have resonances with Buddhism and end with features that contrast with Buddhism.

Question Authority and Rely upon Experiments

It is difficult for modern people to appreciate just how much Aristotle's ideas dominated all areas of intellectual inquiry from aesthetics to science. For centuries, Aristotle's views were so revered that they became for many a straitjacket. Galileo frequently collided with both Aristotelian thinking and church dogma, whether about the nature of pendulums or planetary orbits. Since Galileo's foundation-laying work, modern science cultivates intense skepticism toward authority, whether the authority is Aristotle or Isaac Newton. For example, Newton assumed absolute space and time, that all observers measure the same value for space and time intervals regardless of their states of motion. However, this assumption did not stop Albert Einstein from developing relativity, which shows that the structure of space and time is dependent upon the reference frame of the observer—a topic discussed in detail in a later chapter. Yet I must also note that scientists are often completely unable to turn a skeptical eye toward some of their most cherished beliefs and presuppositions, thereby blocking the advance of knowledge. Unfortunately, such one-sided skepticism is characteristic of nearly all disciplines.

In any case, the final arbiter in science is always experiment. As the famous Nobel Prize–winning physicist Richard Feynman told us, "The principle of science, the definition, almost, is the following: The test of all knowledge is experiment. Experiment is the sole judge of scientific 'truth.'"[9] Thus, following Galileo and Feynman, I just discussed a simple experiment that anybody can do to discover some critical features about the pendulum—independent of any authority. Experiments in science must be controlled, reproducible, and objective, that is, in the public domain. Any qualified experimenter must be able to repeatedly perform the experiment and display the data for others to examine.

Of course, modern experiments in physics are considerably more sophisticated than merely timing the period of a pendulum, and thus becoming a competent experimentalist requires many years of training. Therefore, being in the "public domain" actually means intersubjective agreement among the small community of properly trained physicists. In other words, properly trained experimentalists who share the same commitments about how physics is done must agree on the results of experiments. Because experiments must agree, whether done in Pisa, Lhasa, or Pretoria, science spreads easily across boundaries and can serve as a uniting cultural force. This ability of science to cross national boundaries is enhanced by its being based upon objective analysis independent of religious and cultural views (although science has its own philosophic presuppositions).

An interesting complication occurs when considering the mind itself as a subject of experiment. Take, for example, the development of vivid, one-pointed concentration of the mind on the mind—what Buddhists call *shamatha*. Here there is no object of meditation in the sense of a well-defined content of mind, such as an image or any physical object. As my teacher, Anthony would say, "Focus attention on attention." By this statement he meant that the mind should vividly focus upon itself and not any of its productions, whether thoughts or feelings. Serious practitioners of *shamatha* can reproduce certain results and converse intelligently about them. However, such results are subjective, first-person accounts, which are not objectifiable or in the public domain. Such subjective experiences are repeatable and controlled but not conventional scientific objects.

Let me address more generally how the inbuilt skepticism and devotion to tightly controlled, publicly reproducible experiments in science compare with how Buddhism tests its ideas for validity. At first glance, it seems that, as a religion, Buddhism relies heavily on the authority of its founder and his followers. However, this is not the case. For example, the Dalai Lama writes, "[W]hen it comes to validating the truth of a claim, Buddhism accords greatest authority to experience, with reason second, and Scripture last."[10] We can get a fuller sense of what His Holiness means by briefly reviewing the traditional Buddhist view of the Four Reliances:[11]

1. Rely on the teaching, not the teacher's authority.
2. Rely on the meaning, not the letter.
3. Rely on the definitive meaning, not the interpretable meaning.
4. Rely on the nonconceptual wisdom, not on dualistic cognition.

The first reliance exhorts Buddhists to consider the actual teaching and see if it is coherent, effective, and so forth, independently of whatever reverence we might have for the teacher. Whether the teacher is the original Buddha or the fourteenth Dalai Lama, we should follow the Buddha's advice given in *A Sutra on [Pure Realms] Spread Out in a Dense Array.* For example, the Dalai Lama quoted this *Sutra* with the following words, "Monks and scholars should accept my word not out of respect, but upon analyzing it as a goldsmith analyzes gold, through cutting, melting, scraping, and rubbing it."[12] The second reliance asks us to seek the meaning rather than the literal truth of a statement. In other words, we must get beneath the detailed words used in expressing an idea to the essential meaning embedded in the idea. The third reliance gives more detail on how to interpret the Buddhist teaching. I refer the interested reader to the numerous commentaries on the questions of how these Four Reliances affect the interpretation of religious texts[13] and turn to the fourth reliance, which tells us to rely on nonconceptual wisdom rather than dualistic cognition. Here is the connection to the role of experiments in science.

If we follow the fourth reliance and heed the detailed instructions on meditation and related disciplines, we can perform an experiment with our own minds. Then the truth of the Buddha's message comes through a nonconceptual experience, one grounded in knowledge beyond the categories of language. Although this experiment in the attainment of nonconceptual wisdom is not easy, it is controlled and replicable, as untold numbers of Buddhists have found. Thus, just as in science, "The test of all knowledge is experiment."

Of course, there are some differences, too. Set aside the repeatable and communicable experiences mentioned above in the cultivation of *shamatha* or vivid, one-pointed concentration on the mind. Consider instead the experience of truly nonconceptual knowledge. Such knowledge is nondualistic and cannot be adequately transmitted to another person in dualistic language. Therefore, it is not in the public domain like the content of science. For example, I could explain to the Dalai Lama the details of the physics of pendulums. He could follow the arguments and perform the required experiments to confirm the theory. However, despite the Dalai Lama's skill as a teacher, he will have limited success in describing the experience of the subtle mind or the mind of clear light. Certainly, his words or conceptual formulation will not deliver the experience to the student. Nor could the Dalai Lama fully share his experience of the subtle mind of clear light with the student. Instead, the student has to perform his own experiment and personally and directly experience the subtle mind.

Thus, we can see that, despite the similarities in their attitudes toward authority, reason, and the necessity for empirical verification through experiments, there are significant differences between science and Buddhism. That should hardly be a surprise, given that science is the study of nature in all its forms, while Buddhism is primarily concerned with the alleviation of suffering. Yet, because the root of suffering is our failure to understand the true nature of reality, which includes the domain of science, we can also expect many deep connections between Buddhism and science.

Mathematics and Objectification

From his earliest work onward, Galileo extolled the importance of mathematical formulation. For example, he wrote:

> Philosophy is written in this grand book, the universe, which stands continually open to our gaze. But the book cannot be understood unless one first learns to comprehend the language and to read the alphabet in which it is composed. It is written in the language of mathematics . . . without which it is humanly impossible to understand a single word of it; without these, one wanders about in a dark labyrinth.[14]

In science, if we are not to "wander about in a dark labyrinth," we must mathematically formulate our knowledge. It is important to recall that, to formulate an entity or principle mathematically, it must be precise and fully objective. In this way, we are followers of the famous French philosopher-mathematician René Descartes who exerted such a powerful influence on the early development of science. He advised us to build our theories only from clear and simple ideas, from precisely defined, objective elements. Mathematical formulation clarifies our conceptions and often allows us to deduce unexpected consequences of the theory. The demand for objectification in mathematics means that first-person or subjective accounts of any experience, whether of a toothache or a great mystical achievement, are not permitted. Such accounts are simply not in the public domain. They cannot be verified by another independent observer and thus are not proper data for science.

However, a neuroscientist could measure the brain states of somebody having a toothache or a mystical experience. These data are objective and appropriate for scientific analysis. Yet, the neuroscientist's measurements cannot directly contact the exquisite pain from the dentist's drill or the exquisite bliss and peace of the mystical experience. These aspects of the experience are inevitably subjective and outside of the domain of science. Of course, science could and does change, but today's science is always concerned with the objective.

The emphasis in science on mathematics and objectification contrasts strongly with Buddhism, which makes its final appeal to nondual experience. Such nondual experience cannot be captured through mathematical or linguistic concepts and is certainly a first-person or subjective experience. Although Buddhism has an elaborate and sophisticated philosophical and psychological structure, the final appeal is to a nonconceptual experience, one that does not consist of a well-defined subject relating to an objectifiable content.

This point is so critical that it deserves more discussion. Just from our little knowledge of the pendulum, we can see how a scientific experiment requires objectification. In contrast, I briefly discuss the Buddhist meditation on the nature of mind as a specific example of a nonconceptual knowledge. For example, the Dalai Lama instructs us on how to concentrate on the mind itself. He says:

> Do not let your mind think of what has happened in the past, nor let it chase after things that might happen in the future; rather, leave the mind vivid, without any constructions, just as it is. In this space between old and new ideas, discover the natural, unfabricated, luminous, and knowing nature of the mind unaffected by thought. When you remain this way, you understand that the mind is like a mirror, reflecting any object, any conception, and that the mind has a nature of mere luminosity and knowing, of mere experience.[15]

To apprehend the "mind vivid, without any constructions, just as it is" or to know the "luminous and knowing nature of the mind unaffected by thought" is an experience of identity between the knower and the known. Alternatively, the empirical subject, what we normally take ourselves to be, becomes so attenuated by the cessation of conceptual thinking that it no longer impedes a direct apprehension of the mind. Such knowledge is neither an objectification nor reification. Such a first-person experiment or experience is radically different from scientific knowledge, which must be fully objectifiable and quantifiable. Knowing directly the nature of mind "unaffected by thought" must be nonconceptual, not a content captured in a quantifiable net like a scientific term or principle.

Because such meditation experiences or types of knowledge are so different from knowledge in science, I turn to poets, masters at using words to capture that which is beyond words. For example, consider the poem "Oceans" by Juan Ramón Jiménez, translated by Robert Bly.

> I have a feeling that my boat
> has struck, down there in the depths,
> against a great thing.
> And nothing
> happens! Nothing . . . Silence . . . Waves. . . .
> —Nothing happens? Or has everything happened,
> and are we standing now, quietly, in the new life?[16]

At the risk of defeating poetry with words, a few are in order here. The "great thing" that is struck cannot, from the Buddhist perspective, inherently or independently exist. I interpret it as a reference to the vividness and power accompanying any direct intuition of the mind's sheer luminosity and knowing, not as some concrete object standing on its own in an objective way. This intuition, this kind of direct knowing, is not something that happens in the conventional sense of the word. It is more accurately characterized as silence, nothing happening, waves of thought subsiding into the vastness of mind. Yet, despite the silence and lack of activity, a new life is quietly generated, and we stand in its midst. Although not stated here, such experience is often saturated with great joy or bliss.

On the other hand, as scientists and Buddhists are aware, subjective first-person accounts present difficulties. The following story from the Zen tradition nicely illustrates the difficulty of first-person accounts.

> "Our schoolmaster used to take a nap every afternoon," related a disciple of Soyen Shaku. "We children asked him why he did it and he told us: 'I go to dreamland to meet the old sages just as Confucius did.' When Confucius slept, he would dream of ancient sages and later tell his followers about them.

> "It was extremely hot one day so some of us took a nap. Our schoolmaster scolded us. 'We went to dreamland to meet the ancient sages the same as Confucius did,' we explained. 'What was the message from those sages?' our schoolmaster demanded. One of us replied: 'We went to dreamland and met the sages and asked them if our schoolmaster came there every afternoon, but they said they had never seen any such fellow.'"[17]

Here we not only see quick-witted and insolent students but recognition of the difficulties inherent in first-person accounts. If someone claims to have a profound meditation experience, whether communicating with ancient sages or experiencing the mind of clear light, unlike a scientific content, it is difficult to verify, in the sense in which a scientist uses the term. On the other hand, it really does not take a great deal of sensitivity to appreciate a truly quiet mind, even when you don't have one.

Meaning and Purpose

Essentially all religions are an expression of our deep need for purpose and meaning in life. Buddhism directly addresses this need in its particular way. For example, the Dalai Lama never tires of telling us that the purpose of life is to be happy. He even has books with titles such as *The Meaning of Life* and *How to Practice: The Way to a Meaningful Life*.[18] He gave a particularly direct expression of this view in a speech at the "Forum 2000" conference, Prague, Czech Republic, September 3–7, 1997, where he said, "I believe that the very purpose of life is to be happy. From the very core of our being, we desire contentment. In my own limited experience I have found that the more we care for the happiness of others, the greater is our own sense of well-being."[19]

For many people with a religious outlook or at least an active inner life, the quest for the meaning or purpose in life is a central concern. Personally, I could not justify breathing the air on this planet if I did not have some meaning in my life. Contrast this point of view with that of the reductive scientific materialist—the view that all mental states are expressions of physical states and that all physical states are expressions of the laws of physics. Within this view, spirituality is reduced to psychology, psychology to biology, and biology is, in turn, reduced to chemistry and physics. Therefore, since all matter and fields and everything built upon them are choreographed by the laws of physics, then these laws structure the entire universe in its totality. Of course, not all scientists hold to this point of view. Yet, it is certainly a widespread point of view, if not the majority view.

For an example, I turn to one of its most articulate and brilliant spokespersons, Steven Weinberg, a famous Nobel prize–winning physicist and one of the leading figures in the grand unification project in physics. I have learned much physics from Weinberg and, although I do not always agree with his nontechnical writing, it is always stimulating. In a much quoted statement, he wrote:

> It is almost irresistible for humans to believe that we have some special relation to the universe, that human life is not just a more-or-less farcical outcome of a chain of accidents reaching back to the first three minutes, but that we were somehow built from the beginning. . . . It is hard to realize that this all [i.e., life on earth] is just a tiny part of an overwhelmingly hostile universe. It is even harder to realize that this present universe has evolved from an unspeakably unfamiliar early condition, and faces a future extinction of endless cold or intolerable heat. The more the universe seems comprehensible, the more it also seems pointless.[20]

Elsewhere he says, "The [materialist] reductionist worldview *is* chilling and impersonal. It has to be accepted as it is, not because we like it, but because that is the way the world works."[21] Many people have debated Weinberg and the position he represents. However, if you reduce everything to the functioning of physics, there are certainly no meanings or purposes within the laws of physics. Thus, the materialist reductionist approach must lead to a meaningless or purposeless universe.

Figure 1.5 briefly summarizes the discussion so far in this chapter. The ellipse on the left, representing Buddhism, includes phenomena that are subjective and objective, personal, nonquantifiable, and meaningful. The ellipse on the right, representing science, includes phenomena that are objective, public, quantifiable, and without meaning. As indicated by the overlapping darker region in the center, Buddhism and science have a significant common ground, some of which I explore in this book. While science focuses exclusively on the objective phenomena of nature, Buddhism also has an interest in such phenomena. Despite Buddhism's focus on the inner subjective realm, the Buddhist who would alleviate suffering must also understand the true nature of the objective world. The Buddhist need not understand the details of the outer world, such as the structure of a DNA molecule or the quantum mechanical description of matter, but she must seek to understand the fundamental nature of the physical world. Therefore, she must either be in harmony with science or in disagreement with it.

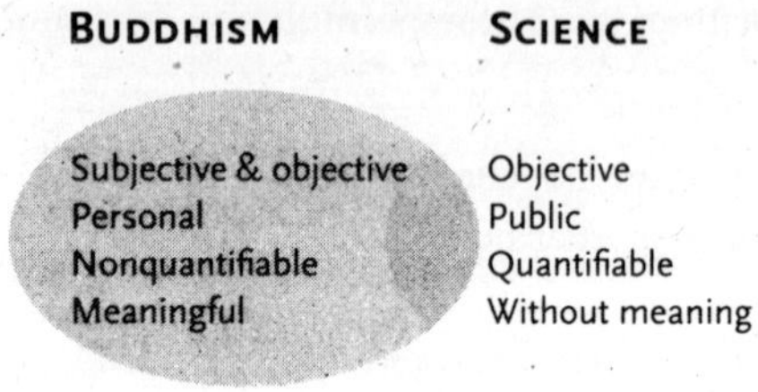

FIGURE 1.5. *Buddhism and science domains*

Many people, the Dalai Lama included,[22] consider science and Buddhism to be complementary investigations. The complementarity we see in quantum mechanics between waves and particles or in Taoism between yin and yang can be a helpful way of understanding the relationship between science and Buddhism. However, this idea can be abused to keep science and Buddhism completely separate from each other. In other words, a scientist might say to the Buddhist, "Fine, you study the subjective, inner, personal realm, and I'll study the objective, impersonal, and public realm. In this way, I'll stay off your turf, and you stay off mine." There are many reasons that this is an unacceptable position. At this stage, we can see it simply will not work because there is a realm where Buddhism and science inevitably collide in their view of objective phenomena.

Personal Transformation and Feelings

Although there is a genuine divergence between science and Buddhism regarding the universality of objectification, both claim that anybody with sufficient talent and motivation could undergo the requisite training and have the confirming experience—whether understanding mathematical theory and its connection to laboratory experiment or the attainment of nonconceptual awareness of ultimate truth. However, in Buddhism this attainment requires a transformation of the personality at the most profound levels. In science, on the other hand, no such transformation of the individual is required. Yes, following the usual route in science through the Ph.D. and into contemporary research does require some native talent and much hard work; however, it does not require any moral and spiritual transformation.

To elaborate on this distinction, let us consider the role of feeling in science and Buddhism. As I write this, students taking my physics course are doing sophisticated calculations using advanced mathematical software and confirming those predictions with laboratory experiment. Along the way, there are innumerable frustrations with the mathematics, the software, and the experimental apparatus. We train the students to eliminate their negative feelings and emotional responses as much as possible. Reacting emotionally only makes problems worse. Despite this truth, often when doing physics on a computer or in the lab, we regrettably engage in anger, threats, and name-calling toward the equipment. Of course, that only makes our frustration worse.

We do try to inspire positive feelings in students by showing them the genuine beauty inherent in the laws of nature, but we never exhort them to take a reverent attitude toward either the science or those who practice it. Yes, we want them to appreciate that there really is beauty in the formulation and the doing of science, but we do not usually encourage any sense of sacredness about it. In short, we attempt to disinfect science of feelings since it might compromise our objectivity, our ability to formulate and confirm the laws of nature independent of our personal preferences, religious commitments, or philosophic predilections.

In contrast, in Buddhism, there is a strong emphasis on cultivating positive feelings and devotion along with refining these critical modes of experience. Buddhists are actually defined by those who take refuge in the Three Jewels: the Buddha, the *dharma*, and the *sangha*. The Buddha, the awakened one, is an exemplar of the tradition. The *dharma* is the Buddha's teachings that can lead us to awakening, while the *sangha* is the community of those who devote themselves to this pursuit of ultimate knowledge. Especially in the Tibetan tradition, the Three Jewels are embodied in the guru toward whom we are advised to cultivate devotion and the most refined of feelings. A typical Tibetan statement reads, "Devotion to the teacher is thus the core of all our spiritual practice, regardless of the particular stages of the path we cultivate. For these reasons, guru yoga is considered the most vital and necessary of all practices and is in itself the surest and fastest way to reach the goal of enlightenment."[23] In contrast, science professors certainly want high marks on the student evaluation of teaching forms that are completed at the end of each course, but we certainly do not consciously encourage "professor yoga" or encourage refinement of feeling as part of science education.

Let me approach this difference in attitude towards feeling in science and Buddhism from another direction. Although I must stress that it is never fully achieved, the ideal in science is to formulate the science and perform the confirming experiments in a completely detached and dispassionate way, free from our personal likes and dislikes, our philosophic and religious preferences, and our race or national identity. These dispassionate ideals contribute to the universality of science.

Here is a concrete example of detached science. Most physics majors in schools throughout the world take a course in modern electronics. Through such electronics and modern computing technology, it is possible to build devices that actually take experimental data without anyone being in the laboratory. Of course, the theory tells us what we can measure and how to interpret our data. Thus, any scientific theory always has a philosophical underpinning. So we never eliminate the human being and her understanding; nevertheless, through computer-controlled data acquisition, we are approaching the ideal of the completely detached observer.

In contrast, the idea of universal compassion, the altruistic activity of relieving the suffering of all sentient beings, is the cornerstone of Buddhism. One of the primary methods of cultivating universal compassion is to develop empathy, which is primarily a function of feeling, of sympathetically connecting to the other suffering being. Here we are trying to make the most intimate feeling connection with the other, just the opposite of the detached observer. The Dalai Lama writes about this deep feeling connection:

> At a basic level, compassion (*nying je*) is understood mainly in terms of empathy—our ability to enter into and, to some extent, share others' suffering. But Buddhists—and perhaps others—believe that this can be developed to such a degree that not only does our compassion arise without any effort, but it is unconditional, undifferentiated, and universal in

> scope. A feeling of intimacy toward all other sentient beings, including of course those who would harm us, is generated, which is likened in the literature to the love a mother has for her only child.[24]

What could be farther from the detached observer or the objective, dispassionate attitude of science?

Levels of Knowledge and Being

Because theoretical physics is so mathematical and abstract, it is often difficult to appreciate that all physics is on one level of being. For example, whether we are formulating the physics of a pendulum or the physics of a quark, it is all done and understood on the same level of being or existence. Yes, the physics of quarks is subtle and abstract and requires much training to be mastered. Yet, each element of the theory is objective and precisely defined. If each element were not fully objective, then it could not be mathematically formulated. Thus, each aspect of the physical theory is on the same level of being as a stone or a flower. Yes, the equations of general relativity or quantum mechanics seem as though they are of a different nature from stones or flowers. The equations require much previous training and are full of abstraction and compact significance. However, when I write the equations on the blackboard or seek their solution for a particular problem, they are just as objective as a red rose. Yes, the dusty chalk on my blackboard does not smell as good as a rose; however, equations or roses are known objectively and can be shared with others. Of course, a theory in physics is verified by its ability to predict the results of carefully controlled experiments, but experiments are on the same level of being as the theory itself. This is such an important point that I want to say it again in a different way by stressing the state of consciousness required to know quarks or roses.

Let us say that an introductory physics student is formulating the physics of a pendulum and verifying the theory in the laboratory. In contrast, let us say that the physics student's teacher is formulating the physics of a nonlocal quantum object and verifying it in a sophisticated modern laboratory. Although the mathematical tools required and the experimental techniques involved in verification are much more sophisticated and abstract for the teacher, neither teacher nor student is required to change their level of consciousness from its ordinary form. In other words, the same state of consciousness that we employ in following the directions to set the time on our new digital watch is the same state, with some concentration and refinement, which we employ in studying pendulums or nonlocal quantum objects. All these objects, whether a watch, a nonlocal quantum object, or a stone, are all on the same level of being, having the same ontological status.

Let us contrast this with the situation in Buddhism. Without appealing to any of the esoteric philosophy or subtle meditation practices of Buddhism, we can just notice that, in the Four Reliances, there are distinct levels of being in Buddhism. In the first reliance, when we are following the Buddha's advice "to analyze and check [his teaching] the way a goldsmith analyzes gold," we are employing the same state of consciousness used in science. On the other hand, following the fourth reliance, the attainment of nonconceptual knowledge, requires an enormous change in our level of being, the fundamental nature of who we are. In short, Buddhism is replete with levels of knowledge and different states of consciousness.

With just this brief review, you can see that there are both striking similarities and divergences between Buddhism and science. Now, what kind of dialogue could occur, and what possible benefits could it yield?

Science and Buddhism in Dialogue

Some topics provide an easier focus for a science and Buddhism dialogue than others. For example, both modern physics and Buddhism take strong and clear positions on such things as space, time, the fundamental nature of matter, and so forth. While their views on these fundamental issues differ, there nevertheless can be areas for fruitful dialogue and examples of the overlap in domains of concern, as diagrammed in figure 1.5 above. Other topics are more problematic. Whereas Buddhism, for example, has a clear and sophisticated view of the nature of mind, there is no widely accepted view of the fundamental nature of mind in modern science: the diversity of views in modern science about the nature of mind makes a dialogue with Buddhism on this topic difficult. Even more fundamentally, the general objective characteristic of scientific knowledge exacerbates the problem. For example, science focuses upon states of mind or contents of mind (third-person accounts, not first-person accounts), rather than the innate and subjective nature of mind. Despite such difficulties, interesting collaborations are still possible.

Let me give a concrete example. Because anger is such an enemy of compassion, Buddhism has much to say about the topic. From a scientific point of view, anger has many physiological and psychological components that are susceptible to quantification and measurement, such as changes in blood pressure, heart rate, brain signals, and so forth. We can thus immediately see that anger would be a relatively easy topic for Buddhists and scientists to discuss together. Here is an area for real collaboration and mutual stimulation.

As a contrasting example, consider the fundamental nature of all objective and subjective phenomena as empty, as totally lacking independent or inherent existence. I will not take time now to discuss the nature of Buddhist emptiness in detail, something done in later chapters, but just ask the reader to understand emptiness as the fundamental nature or the ultimate truth of all phenomena. For the subtle mind or the mind of clear light to know the emptiness of phenomena requires a fusion or interpenetration of the mind and emptiness. The Buddhist texts often describe this knowing as being like water flowing into water. Clearly, such nonconceptual knowledge, such knowledge by identity, rather than objectification, would be a very difficult area for a science and Buddhism dialogue.

Given that some topics are more difficult than others as a basis for dialogue and that there are major differences between modern science and Buddhism, as sketched in the previous section, what can we expect from such a dialogue? Of course, the greatest proponent and pioneer of the science and Buddhism dialogue has been the Dalai Lama. He has invested much time and energy into the dialogue. I therefore turn to his writings, in particular to *The Universe in a Single Atom*, for partial answers to this question.

In this book, the Dalai Lama makes a statement he has often made in the past about how Buddhism may be influenced by science. He writes, "My confidence in venturing into science lies in my basic belief that as in science so in Buddhism, understanding the nature of reality is pursued by means of critical investigation: if scientific analysis were conclusively to demonstrate certain claims in Buddhism to be false, then we must accept the findings of science and abandon those claims."[25] For example, there are certain traditional texts studied in the Tibetan monasteries that clearly have outdated ideas according to modern cosmology and physics. The Dalai Lama suggests that these texts be revised. He writes, "Certainly some specific aspects of Buddhist thought—such as its old cosmological theories and its rudimentary physics—will have to be modified in the light of new scientific insights."[26] Here we see science as a modernizer of Buddhism. Of course, such an approach warms the heart of any scientist—especially today when so many fundamentalists want to revise science according to their religious beliefs.

Now the question immediately arises whether Buddhism can have a reciprocal influence upon science. This question can be asked in two parts. First, can Buddhism influence the content and practice of science? For example, Buddhism has a great deal to say about various mental states, whether anger or happiness, and the study of such states can provide knowledge and stimulus for science. As a concrete example, consider the effect of meditation upon the brain. Recent measurements on the brains of meditators have shown that there are significant differences attributable to meditation.[27] This is clearly a fruitful area for collaboration and for future research. The Dalai Lama gives other examples of such fruitful areas for interaction between science and Buddhism.

An example central to this book focuses upon the radical change in our worldview that comes from understanding the implications of quantum mechanics and relativity. Although there are controversial areas in the philosophic and conceptual interpretation of quantum mechanics (less so in relativity), I focus entirely on topics where there is wide general agreement. My interpretations of quantum mechanics and relativity are very much in the main stream; yet, as we will see, the topics I discuss provide a drastically different view of the world and our relationship to it than the one we conventionally hold. Unfortunately, this new view has not worked its way into our collective understanding of nature, even in the most scientifically advanced countries, where we still cling to the old Newtonian view of a world of independently existent objects. Therefore, modern physics has not transformed our worldview to the extent that it should. Here, Buddhist philosophy, especially the understanding of emptiness, is of enormous help in both clarifying the physical ideas and pointing out their moral implications.

The second way to ask this question about reciprocal influence of Buddhism on science is more difficult precisely because it focuses upon the moral implications and injunctions of Buddhism. The Dalai Lama writes, "The central question—central for the survival and well-being of our world—is how we can make the wonderful developments of science into something that offers altruistic and compassionate service for the needs of humanity and the other sentient beings with whom we share this earth."[28] Here the Dalai Lama is suggesting that Buddhism can offer moral guidance for science and its applications in technology. He frequently returns to this theme. For example, he is especially concerned about the grave and far-reaching moral challenges presented by our growing ability to manipulate the fundamental genetic structure of life. However, from my experience of the scientific community, I can say that the vast majority of scientists do not want any influence from the outside, whether from Buddhism, philosophy, or politics. For example, Steven Weinberg writes, "I know of *no one* who has participated actively in the advance of physics in the postwar period whose research has been significantly helped by the work of philosophers."[29]

Resistance to outside influences on science comes from more than just working scientists. I have often discussed with students the enormous moral challenges presented to us by science and its associated technology. Whether we are speaking about weapons of mass destruction, genetic engineering, or the varied and profound ecological crises at hand, science needs moral guidance. However, some of my brightest students believe that science is the only legitimate search for truth and that it should proceed unhindered, without any constraints from Buddhism or any other outside influence. This view, although not universal, comes from bright students majoring in all disciplines. Their argument is that science does not need guidance, but the people who employ science need guidance. I find this very troubling—largely because these students, along with many practitioners of science, believe that science is the sole arbiter of truth, that which tells us what is actual and real. Despite the limitations of the scientific point of view, some of which I have reviewed in the previous section, many cling to science as "the one true religion." I believe this scientific fundamentalism is profoundly misguided and a grave danger to our planet.

Despite these experiences, I fully agree with the Dalai Lama about the ability of Buddhism to provide moral guidance for science and agree that science is necessary for our very survival as a species. Therefore, in this book I take up the challenge of showing how moral implications flow naturally from the worldview implied by modern physics and that these moral implications are not extrinsic or a foreign imposition on science.

Finally, I believe that the most important reason for engaging in the science and Buddhism dialogue is that it can be a powerful expression of the *bodhisattva* vow—the unswerving commitment to work for the relief of suffering for all sentient beings. We are all aware of the overwhelming power of science and technology to shape our world, to affect our lives, and to bring great suffering or joy to the human race. The same is true for religion, which has a similar power to do great good or equally great evil. Whether you have taken the *bodhisattva* vow or not, it is easy to see that the Dalai Lama understands that the science and Buddhism collaboration is an expression of that vow. This view is especially clear in the last paragraph of *The Universe in a Single Atom*, from which I quoted a small part earlier. There, because of the great challenges facing humanity, the Dalai Lama pleads for all of us to engage in this dialogue:

> Since the emergence of modern science, humanity has lived through an engagement between spirituality and science as two important sources of knowledge and well-being. Sometimes the relationship has been a close one—a kind of friendship—while at other times it has been frosty, with many finding the two to be incompatible. Today, in the first decade of the twenty-first century, science and spirituality have the potential to be closer than ever, and to embark upon a collaborative endeavor that has far-reaching potential to help humanity meet the challenges before us. We are all in this together. May each of us, as a member of the human family, respond to the moral obligation to make this collaboration possible. This is my heartfelt plea.[30]

2. Quantum Mechanics and Compassion

Parallels and Problems

Anthony Damiani often showed us how a good problem or question can be more valuable than a good answer. My own inner experience—along with nearly four decades of academic teaching and research—confirms that perspective: whether in theoretical physics, Buddhism, or the psychology of C. G. Jung, focusing on sources of confusion always drives me into fertile territory and creative possibilities. I approach this chapter in that spirit.

The exploration begins with a fundamental principle in quantum mechanics and ends with a remarkable development of a parallel principle in Tibetan Buddhism. I never argue that quantum mechanics in any way proves the truths of Buddhism. Rather, I am considering a deep similarity in their respective approaches to indistinguishability, the establishment of it through exchange, and the consequences that flow from it. This similarity forces me to confront my selfishness and wrestle with the demand for universal compassion that arises from the Tibetan Buddhist version of indistinguishability. My approach through a physics and Buddhism parallel offers a unique perspective on compassion, the other great pillar alongside of emptiness upon which Tibetan Buddhism stands.

Uniqueness and Indistinguishability in Physics

As a child, I loved the game of marbles. My pockets often bulged and rattled with brightly colored glass spheres. A circle drawn in the dirt with marbles placed in it, knuckles on the ground with a marble tucked into the pocket in front of my thumbnail, and off we go blasting marbles out of the circle. I had a wicked shot. We all had our favorite "shooter" and preferred certain colors and designs of marbles to others.

Imagine putting ten marbles into a box and then vigorously shaking it. The marbles bounce off each other and the walls of the box in complicated ways. Nevertheless, thanks to their differing colors and designs, we know that each marble has a unique identity. We also know that each particle has a well-defined trajectory in the box, no matter how complex the motion or how many marbles are in the box. Therefore, if we filmed the marbles as they bounced around in the box, we could easily distinguish cases in which the marbles were exchanged. For example, we would have no trouble distinguishing the film in which the red marble starts in the left corner and the black marble starts in the right corner from the film in which the starting positions of the red and black marbles were exchanged. However, the situation is entirely different in quantum mechanics.

The simplest system showing how different things are in quantum mechanics is a box containing two electrons. (You could also use protons, neutrons, or whatever elementary particles you like, as long as they are of the same kind.) With marbles in the back of our minds, we imagine a little number "1" engraved on one electron and a number "2" engraved on the other—signifying the unique identity of the electrons. Of course, you cannot engrave electrons, but they do have different physical properties. A minimal description of these properties must consider the particle's location and quantum mechanical spin. (Quantum mechanical spin has no exact macroscopic analogue, but we can approximate it by thinking of the spin of a top or wheel that rotates with constant speed. Although the value of the quantum mechanical spin does not change, its orientation relative to a designated set of coordinate axes does.) With our experience with marbles in mind, we assume that the physical property set uniquely defines the electron, giving it a well-defined identity. Furthermore, we imagine that it is possible to follow the path of particles 1 and 2 inside the box, tracing out their separate trajectories. However, our experience with marbles has led us astray here.

In contrast to marbles, electrons or other elementary particles do not have well-defined trajectories despite the continuous evolution of the system. Even more important for my present purposes, the two electrons are completely indistinguishable. That is, mathematically exchanging properties for particle 1 with those of particle 2 leads to no discernable change in the system, no measurable differences. Although the mathematical exchange of particle properties is clearly defined, it results in *no mea-*

surable differences. We have a clear conceptual difference (mathematical exchange of properties) without empirical or measurable consequences.

From the point of view of macroscopic experience, this indistinguishability established through exchange in quantum mechanics is a very strange idea. Yet, it is an absolutely fundamental principle. So it is worth stating the physics more precisely. In box A, place electron e1, with well-defined properties or attributes P_1 (P_1 must minimally contain a specification of the location and spin of the electron). Let electron e_2 have properties P_2. Now in box B exchange the properties so that P_1 becomes P_2 and P_2 becomes P1 (see figure 2.1 below). No measurements of *any kind* on boxes A and B can distinguish any differences between these boxes. In short, *indistinguishability of quantum particles means that exchanging particle properties has no measurable effect.*

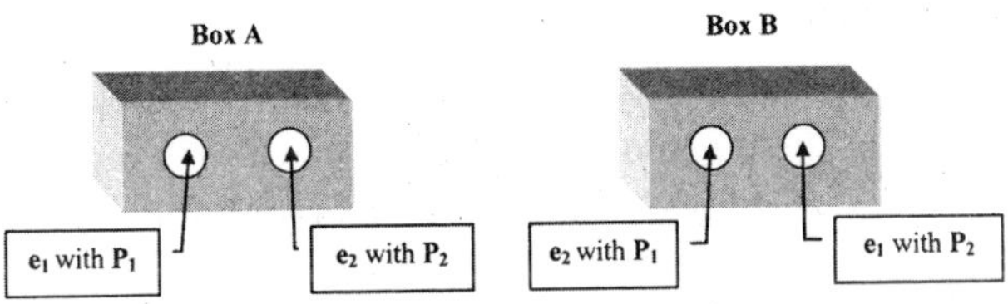

FIGURE 2.1. *Experimentally indistinguishable configurations*

Whether we have a box with two or two trillion electrons in it, we have the erroneous tendency to believe that each electron has a well-defined or unique identity, an essence or self-nature, a sort of "serial number" stamped on it. In fact, as particle exchanges reveals, all of the electrons in a given system are completely indistinguishable—without an essence or self-nature. Furthermore, the indistinguishable particles do not have well-defined paths or trajectories and yet the system evolves continuously from one state to the next.

As we will see in later chapters, here is the typical situation in quantum mechanics where we have continuity without self-nature, continuous evolution of the system without any unique or independently existing essence to the objects undergoing the evolution. The next chapter has a remarkable Buddhist reflection of this principle. There we will see how the Middle Way appreciates the unique nature of each individual and their continuity without there being any inherent self-nature of persons or things. For example, there is a continuity of personal *karma* or action, and you will become a unique buddha, but all this happens without there being any unique self of persons or inherently existing identity. This is a subtle view that combines uniqueness within a thoroughgoing denial of inherent nature of persons. As we will see in several chapters of this book, continuity without a unique identity or self-nature is a core principle within both the Middle Way and quantum mechanics.

The indistinguishability of quantum particles is one of the most fundamental properties of matter. It is a radical departure from classical or Newtonian physics and ordinary experience, where we take for granted the unique identity of the individual elements of our experience, whether they be marbles or people. To see how radical a departure this is from our conventional views, consider the following simple thought experiment. Imagine that we are in a big auditorium with a thousand people. You and I are sitting next to each other. If we exchange seats, could a camera mounted in the ceiling detect any difference in the room?

The camera could take two photographs, one before we switched seats and one after. These photos could be compared with a computer and the differences would easily show up. Even beyond the physical identity detected by a camera, we have an instinctive belief in our unique identity or individual self, something beyond the camera's reach. The emptiness doctrine, discussed in the following chapter, denies this unique identity or self, while acknowledging a conventional identity enshrined in the identification in our wallet. (Recall that the negative formulation of emptiness asserts that all persons and things lack independent or inherent existence, while the positive formulation asserts that phenomena only exist through their interdependence or relatedness.)

In striking contrast to our experience in the auditorium, if you had one thousand electrons in a system and exchanged the property sets of any two particles, there would be no measurable change of any kind. This complete indistinguishability means that there is no individual identity for any of the particles. They are all the same in a deep sense, beyond anything we experience in the macroscopic realm. In other words, each elementary particle is completely empty of a self nature, or they have no inherent existence. Yet, they still function to make atoms, molecules, and the material world within which we live.

The indistinguishability of particles of a given type in a well-defined system is an essential building stone in the foundation of quantum mechanics. It applies to the earliest moments of the big bang and the farthest galaxies. With just a couple of lines of mathematics, this quantum indistinguishability leads directly to the famous Pauli exclusion principle, which says that no two electrons in the same system can occupy the same quantum state. The Pauli principle accounts for the stability of the matter making up our bodies and the rest of the universe. It also accounts for the detailed spectra of atoms and the structure of the periodic table of the elements.

It should be kept in mind that, for macroscopic systems with large numbers of particles, most quantum effects disappear. *Nevertheless, for a given system, one that can be approximately isolated from the rest of the universe, the particles of a given type are indistinguishable, independent of their number.*

It fills me with wonder to think that the extraordinary multiplicity and diversity seen all around us spring from a sea of indistinguishable elementary particles, entities without a unique identity or self. For the next section, try to keep in the forefront of your mind that there is an intimate connection between exchange of particle properties and indistinguishability. In fact, in quantum mechanics, the lack of measurable differences after exchange establishes indistinguishability, gives us our working definition of what we mean by it, and allows us to draw far-reaching conclusions from indistinguishability. Next, I explore how indistinguishability is realized through exchange in Tibetan Buddhism and see what vital principle flows from it.

Indistinguishability in Tibetan Buddhism

I am sitting on the porch of my favorite cafe, sipping coffee and reading a book. I occasionally look up and watch people coming and going. I never tire of savoring the uniqueness of each individual—all those different sizes, shapes, colors, ways of moving, and unique psychologies. What a delight! There has never been anybody exactly like the reader or writer of this sentence. Starting from the big bang and continuing to the death of the universe, there will never be another person exactly like you. For this reason, each person's path to buddhahood must also be unique. The uniqueness of our path is one reason for the importance of having a guru or lama who can provide individual instruction.

Despite our extraordinary uniqueness, which on the conventional level is never in dispute, there are fundamental ways in which we are all alike. In fact, being dazzled by the uniqueness and multiplicity all around us, there is a real danger that we will fail to appreciate in what ways we are indistinguishable.

Tibetan Buddhism never tires of telling us that everyone desires happiness and freedom from suffering. Yes, you are certainly different from me in innumerable, important ways. However, in that both of us desire happiness and freedom from suffering, we are totally indistinguishable. There are, of course, other ways in which we are alike, but none more fundamental or important than our common desire for happiness and freedom from suffering and our equal right to such happiness. In analogy with physics, if we exchanged any two people and could measure their desire for happiness and freedom from suffering and their right to such happiness, we would find no measurable differences between the states before or after the exchange. Please remember that Buddhism affirms our conventional identity, enshrined in our passport number, but also emphasizes our fundamental indistinguishability in that we all desire happiness and freedom from suffering and have an equal right to such happiness. Here I explore some implications of our indistinguishability.

This type of indistinguishable nature is obvious for most of us. For Americans it has a special resonance because our Declaration of Independence tell us, "We hold these truths to be self-evident, that all men are created equal, that they are endowed by their Creator with certain unalienable Rights, that among these are Life, Liberty and the pursuit of Happiness." Although this self-evident truth in the declaration is not fully upheld and there are differences between it and the Tibetan view of our indistinguishable natures, the fundamental point is the same. Being such an obvious truth, we are in danger of trivializing it or considering it true merely by definition. As we will see, agreeing with Tibetan Buddhism that such indistinguishability of persons is a fundamental truth leads to some powerful implications, at least as significant as the Pauli exclusion principle.

Our common desire for happiness and freedom from suffering is easy to appreciate in the case of our family and loved ones. However, if it is universally true, it must cut across all our likes, dislikes, national boundaries, historical eras, and so forth. For example, even the most hated person or evil tyrant also desires happiness and freedom from suffering. Whether Attila the Hun, a terrorist bomber, or Mother Teresa of Calcutta, we are all the same in this sense. In Tibetan Buddhism, this level of indistinguishability is at least as important as the indistinguishability of particles in quantum mechanics because it is the foundation for universal compassion. Universal compassion, the heart of Tibetan Buddhism, is the sincere desire for the welfare of all sentient beings along with the will to act on this desire. Being universal, it extends far beyond the little circle of our loved ones. In the face of this indistinguishability and its logical consequence of compassion, it is rationally indefensible to act selfishly, to put our needs before those of another. The Dalai Lama tells us:

> Whether people are beautiful and friendly or unattractive and disruptive, ultimately they are human beings, just like oneself. Like oneself, they want happiness and do not want suffering. Furthermore, their right to overcome suffering and be happy is equal to one's own. Now, when you recognize that all beings are equal in both their desire for happiness and their right to obtain it, you automatically feel empathy and closeness for them. Through accustoming your mind to this sense of universal altruism, you develop a feeling of responsibility for others: the wish to help them actively overcome their problems. Nor is this wish selective; it applies equally to all.[1]

Unfortunately, I am not completely ruled by reason or logic. My self-cherishing, my egotism, overwhelms my understanding of our indistinguishable desire for happiness and freedom from suffering. Yet, all the great Tibetan teachers tell us that our self-love, our continuous concern for our ego and its desires, is actually the greatest impediment to our happiness, while love and concern for others are the greatest sources of joy and satisfaction. For example, Shantideva, the eighth-century Indian adept and one of the brightest lights in the firmament of Tibetan Buddhism, tells us:

> Whatever joy there is in this world
> All comes from desiring others to be happy,
> And whatever suffering there is in this world
> All comes from desiring myself to be happy.[2]

For all these years, I had it all wrong. I thought the more attention I paid to my desires and material comforts the happier I would be. Yet, even now that I have some understanding and experience of Shantideva's wisdom, selflessness is not fully a part of my being. I am not always able to actualize this knowledge in my everyday activity. Knowing this, Shantideva gives special exercises that help us overcome our selfishness and realize our fundamental indistinguishability. He wrote:

> Thus whoever wishes to quickly afford protection
> To both himself and other beings
> Should practice that holy secret:
> The exchanging of self for others.[3]

So, just as in quantum mechanics, to establish or realize indistinguishability, we must engage in exchange. Unfortunately, "that holy secret: the exchanging of self for others" is much more difficult than exchanging elementary particle properties. The mathematics necessary to exchange particle properties is simple, and, of course, it helps that emotionally we do not care which particle is which. We simply do not identify with electrons or protons. However, we have spent innumerable incarnations identifying with an ego and its associated body, believing it to be real or independently existent, and focusing on satisfying its insatiable desires. This identification or self-grasping, the false belief in an independently existent ego, immediately gives rise to self-cherishing or egotism. This process is so ingrained, so immediate, that exchanging our self-love for love of another is extremely difficult. Despite this difficulty, we can realize indistinguishability in both physics and Tibetan Buddhism through the procedure of exchange. To help us with the more difficult exchange in Buddhism, Shantideva gives us a powerful exercise with detailed instructions on just how to manipulate our imagination. The exercise takes the following form.

Generally, we break up humanity into three groups: those people that we believe are inferior to us; those that we believe are equal to us and therefore rivals; and, finally, those that we believe are superior to us. The basis for this grouping—whether spiritual attainment, education, money, or other criteria—varies from one person to the next. However, the threefold grouping always occurs. We feel haughty toward our inferiors in the first group, competitive toward our equals in the second, and envious of our superiors in the third. In this exercise, we take the point of view of somebody in the group we believe to be inferior to us. We imaginatively exchange identities with that inferior person. We assume his point of view as much as possible, then gaze back at ourselves through his eyes with envy and criticize ourselves from his point of view.

Let me give an example that would be appropriate for a professor. In our example, the professor thinks very highly of himself, his developed intellect, his ability to articulate and manipulate ideas, and so forth. Let us say that he frequently deals with a secretary who gives him some trouble. Of course, he secretly believes that secretaries are a lesser form of life. Then, implementing Shantideva's exercise, our professor imaginatively takes on the secretary's identity and writes out something like:

> I have so much work. I can never get caught up and he [the professor] just keeps dumping it on my desk and complaining that I'm not fast enough. He's never satisfied with either the quality or quantity of my work. I'm always so tense when I have to leave early to take care of one of my children when they're ill or have to go to a doctor. On top of it all, he often makes disparaging remarks about women. But I need to pay my bills and must do my best with this job. He went to all those fancy schools and has had all the advantages that I never had. He's arrogant, self-centered, and swollen with his own self-importance. He never takes the slightest notice of my needs or appreciates anything I do. Despite all his education and academic honors, he knows nothing about simple kindness.

Of course, such a hopeless professor is unlikely to do this exercise, but I trust you get the general idea. Although Shantideva does not tell us to write out such an exchange, I find writing makes the experience much more concrete and powerful than just doing it entirely in the imagination. When I lectured on material from this chapter at Namgyal Monastery in Ithaca, New York, the former head resident teacher there, Lharampa Geshe Thupten Kunkhen, agreed that writing it out was a good idea. After doing so, you can then take it into your meditation and further deepen the experience.

In Shantideva's description of the imaginative exercise he uses "I" for the person believed inferior and "he" for the practitioner of this exercise (you and me). Taking on the identity of the inferior person, we are to say:

> "He is honored, but I am not;
> I have not found wealth such as he.

He is praised, but I am despised;
He is happy, but I suffer."

"I have to do all the work
While he remains comfortably at rest.
He is renowned as great in this work, but I as inferior
With no good qualities at all."[4]

(Unfortunately, this whining sounds like me on a bad day!) Shantideva then wants us to criticize our self from the point of view of this inferior person. For example, the inferior one criticizes our lack of compassion by saying:

"With no compassion for the beings
Who dwell in the poisonous mouth of evil realms,
Externally he is proud of his good qualities
And wishes to put down the wise."[5]

In essence, then, Shantideva is asking us vividly to take the point of view of somebody we feel is inferior to us and, from this position, generate jealousy and criticism toward ourselves. Depending upon whom you consider your inferior, you modify the exact words to generate the necessary jealousy and criticism toward yourself.

Next, we take the viewpoint of somebody we consider our equal or rival. From that person's viewpoint, we generate intense competitiveness and criticize ourselves from our rival's point of view.

Finally, we take the point of view of somebody we believe is our superior and, from that position, make some withering criticisms of our self and promise to deny ourselves happiness. It is not clear how this person is truly superior when he says about us:

"Even though he has some possessions,
If he is working for me,
I shall give him just enough to live on
And by force I'll take (the rest)."

"His happiness and comfort will decline
And I shall always cause him harm,
For hundreds of times in this cycle of rebirth
He has caused harm to me."[6]

In quantum mechanics we switch particle properties, while in this exercise we switch our self-cherishing or our self-love from its usual location in our body-mind complex to a new location in somebody we believe is inferior, equal, or superior to ourselves. From these three differing viewpoints, we generate intense jealousy, competitiveness, and haughtiness. Then, we criticize ourselves from these three viewpoints. By doing this exercise with concentration and vividness, we learn to take the other person's point of view. We thereby reduce our intense identification with our own point of view and actually make the exchange of self with other. Along with refining our personality, we decrease our false sense that we inherently or independently exist—the root of all our suffering, as the Tibetans never tire of telling us. I encourage you to take a few minutes, identify a person in each of the three groups, and write out an example of the exercise. It may not be entertaining, but it is transformative.

As the excellent commentary on Shantideva's text, *Meaningful to Behold* by Geshe Kelsang Gyatso, tells us:

> The main purpose of such meditative techniques is to stabilize and increase our actual ability to exchange self for others and thereby destroy our self-cherishing. From such an exchange, an unusually strong mind of great compassion emerges and from this, we develop an unusually strong *bodhichitta* motivation [the altruistic desire for enlightenment for the sake of all sentient beings]. In fact, the *bodhichitta* developed by this approach is generally more powerful than that cultivated in the sevenfold cause and effect meditation [discussed in an earlier chapter].[7]

It is important to notice that, by exchanging our identity for that of the other person, the negative states such as jealousy, haughtiness, or criticism are directed at ourselves. In contrast, if we directed these negative states at another person, this would be a form of black magic—the opposite of *bodhisattva* activity. (The *bodhisattva* ideal is to seek liberation to be maximally effective in relieving suffering for all sentient beings.) If our concentration is strong, such directed negative thought would harm the other person. However, even if our concentration is weak, such activity would certainly harm us.

In Shantideva's exercise, a vivid manipulation of our imagination replaces the mathematical manipulations in quantum mechanics. Rather than mathematically exchanging particle properties to reveal the indistinguishability between particles, here we imaginatively exchange our self-cherishing and viewpoint with that of another to realize our fundamental indistinguishability. Through repeated use of this exercise, we can actually learn to exchange self with other and thereby directly experience our fundamental indistinguishability—that everyone desires happiness and freedom from suffering. Then, despite individual differences among us, this indistinguishability becomes a living reality that transforms our world and us. Just as critically important properties of matter arise from quantum indistinguishability, genuine *bodhichitta* arises from our human indistinguishability. Effective use of the exercise of exchanging self with other can transform an unfelt and ineffective truth into one that powerfully guides our every action. In this way, the Tibetans unite love and knowledge.

The Obligations of Compassion

Let us say that through exchanging self with other, the truth of our indistinguishability becomes a living reality, not just a parroted slogan. If despite our obvious differences, we truly realize that, in terms of wanting happiness and freedom from suffering, we are as indistinguishable from each other as elementary particles are, that the truth is just as universal as indistinguishability is in physics, that it applies to all persons from the earliest moments of human history to the present moment, then heavy obligations fall on us. How then can I continue to live a life of luxury when there is so much suffering in the world? How can I rationalize my material indulgences when there are so many who go to bed hungry every night? For example, the most recent report available shows that in 2002 more than 840 million people in the world are undernourished—799 million of them are from the developing world. More than 153 million of them are under the age of five.[8] (For comparison, there are 300 million people in the United States, about 4.6% of the world's total.)

In contrast, 67 percent of U.S. citizens aged twenty and above are overweight and 32 percent are obese, according to the 2003–2004 National Health and Nutrition Examination Survey from the U.S. Center for Disease Control.[9] Given these facts, how can I hold to the indistinguishability of every human and still rationalize my selfish use of resources?

An analysis by the internationally known philosopher and ethicist

Peter Singer provides a particularly vivid formulation of this moral problem.[10] I follow Singer and begin the analysis with a little story.

There is a shallow pond on the Colgate campus with geese, ducks, and beautiful landscaping. One day I am walking past the pond on my way to my Tibet class, and I notice that a little girl has fallen into the water and is drowning. I jump into the pond and pull her out. Of course, my muddy clothes force me to go home and change them and thereby miss class, but everybody agrees that I did the right thing. If there had been other people near the pond who just ignored the girl's drowning, that situation would not absolve me of my responsibility to help her.

After going home and changing my clothes, I return to my office. I check my mail and notice an appeal from Oxfam International. They are soliciting funds for food relief for the masses of people starving in Darfur, Sudan. I feel swamped by requests for aid of all kinds. My regular bills are piling up, and I am saving money for a new car. I throw the request into the recycling bin. Everybody understands my plight. Nobody condemns me.

But wait! Don't the starving people in Darfur want happiness and freedom from suffering just as much as the little drowning girl? Is my compassion only local and not universal—extending to just those physically near me or my loved ones? Today, when news and images of Darfur are just a mouse click away, am I only obliged to help the little drowning girl and not starving Africans? When a few mouse clicks will take $100 from my credit card and efficiently turn it into sustenance for hungry Africans, is spending the same money at a fancy restaurant morally neutral?

I am not alone in my refusal to help the less fortunate abroad, to act on the realization that indistinguishability extends way beyond my little circle of loved ones. For example, averaging over the years 2002 to 2005, the United States is the member of the Development Assistance Committee (DAC) that gives the smallest fraction of its Gross National Income (GNI) for Official Development Assistance (ODA) or what used to be called foreign aid. Figure 2.2 below displays the most recent percentage of ODA to GNI by country for 2005 and shows that the United States is now second from the bottom.[11] This modest improvement is largely through debt relief and aid to war-torn Iraq and Afghanistan, not increases in ODA to the neediest. Since the United States' "war on terror" and related foreign policy initiatives are responsible for the increase in ODA, the true situation is worse than even the dramatic graph reveals. There are many complexities surrounding ODA, which I cannot discuss here. The sad point is that "rich countries give less than half the amount of aid they gave in the early 1960s when they were far less affluent."[12] It pains me as an American to examine figure 2.2 and see how poorly the United States compares to the twenty-one other countries in the DAC. The pain of all this is intensified through practicing exchanging self with other and getting a little taste of the indistinguishability I share with everybody, including those starving in Africa.

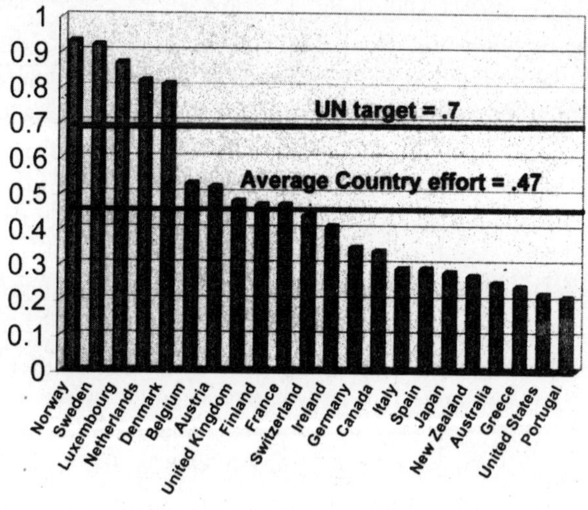

FIGURE 2.2. *ODA as a percentage of GNI by country in 2005*

This yawning divide between rich and poor is a worldwide problem that has doubled in the last decade. Former World Bank president James Wolfensohn tells us:

> Today you have 20 percent of the world controlling 80 percent of the gross domestic product. You've got a $30 trillion economy and $24 trillion of it in the developed countries. The income of the top 20 is 37 times the income of the bottom 20, and it has *doubled in the last decade*. These inequities cannot exist.[13]

In the face of these inequalities, Peter Singer formulates our responsibility when he writes:

> My next point is this: if it is in our power to prevent something bad from happening, without thereby sacrificing anything of comparable moral importance, we ought, morally, to do it. By "without sacrificing anything of comparable moral importance," I mean without causing anything else comparably bad to happen, or doing something that is wrong in itself, or failing to promote some moral good, comparable in significance to the bad thing that we can prevent. This principle seems almost as uncontroversial as the last one [suffering and death from lack of food, shelter, and medical care are bad]. It requires us only to prevent what is bad, and to promote what is good, and it requires this of us only when we can do it without sacrificing anything that is, from the moral point of view, comparably important.[14]

Singer compresses and slightly qualifies his statement by saying, "if it is in our power to prevent something very bad from happening, without thereby sacrificing anything morally significant, we ought, morally, to do it." He points out some of the consequences of his reasoning saying:

> The uncontroversial appearance of the principle just stated is deceptive. If it were acted upon, even in its qualified form, our lives, our society, and our world would be fundamentally changed. For the principle takes, firstly, no account of proximity or distance. It makes no moral difference whether the person I can help is a neighbor's child ten yards from me or a Bengali whose name I shall never know, ten thousand miles away. Secondly, the principle makes no distinction between cases in which I am the only person who could possibly do anything and cases in which I am just one among millions in the same position.[15]

If we accept the truth of our indistinguishability, that everyone desires happiness and freedom from suffering, these conclusions follow with remorseless logic. However, when I presented this argument to students in my Tibet class, they argued that is it different when the person is drowning or hungry right in front of you. Your obligation is obvious and much more compelling then when it is at a distance. Despite being proficient users of the Internet, proximity in terms of mouse clicks is not the same for them as physical proximity.

However, a universal principle such as the indistinguishable nature of electrons must apply in the big bang and in a distant galaxy just as it does in my own body, from my birth to my death. In the same way, our common desire for happiness and freedom from suffering must apply at all times and places; otherwise, it is not a universal principle. Singer is certainly clear about this. Perhaps spending so many years in physics dealing with universal principles and appreciating how they must always apply in all cases intensifies my problem. If I accept our human indistinguishability as a universal principle, it leaves me nowhere to hide from its moral demands.

Nor is there anywhere to hide from the realization of how far I fall short of the *bodhisattva* ideal. Yes, as Professor Lars English of Dickinson College reminds me, a Buddhist believes that prayer and teaching Buddhism, not just sharing material wealth, are important forms of expressing the *bodhisattva* ideal. However, as the quotation below shows, although the Dalai Lama prays fervently for the welfare of all sentient beings and teaches ceaselessly, he believes material help is also required. His Holiness certainly knows the demands of our indistinguishability. He writes:

> I feel strongly that luxurious living is inappropriate, so much so that I must admit that whenever I stay in a comfortable hotel and see others eating and drinking expensively while outside there are people who do not even have anywhere to spend the night, I feel greatly disturbed. It reinforces my feeling that I am no different from either the rich or the poor. We are the same in wanting happiness and not to suffer. And we have an equal right to that happiness. As a result, I feel that if I were to see a workers' demonstration going by, I would certainly join in. And yet, of course, the person who is saying these things is one of those enjoying the comforts of the hotel. Indeed, I must go further. It is also true that I possess several valuable wristwatches. And while I sometimes feel that if I were to sell them I could perhaps build some huts for the poor, so far I have not. In the same way, I do feel that if I were to observe a strictly vegetarian diet not only would I be setting

> a better example, but I would also be helping to save innocent animals' lives. Again, so far I have not and therefore must admit a discrepancy between my principles and my practice in certain areas. At the same time, I do not believe everyone can or should be like Mahatma Gandhi and live the life of a poor peasant. Such dedication is wonderful and greatly to be admired. But the watchword is "As much as we can"—without going to extremes.[16]

Here we see the Dalai Lama's deep commitment to our indistinguishable nature, to our equal right to happiness and freedom from suffering. However, given that even the Dalai Lama, the *bodhisattva* of compassion, admits "a discrepancy between my principles and my practice in certain areas," where does this leave those of us struggling against our selfishness to develop *bodhichitta*? Sadly, I do not have an answer, only the awareness of my shortcomings and a resolve to improve. That resolve partly expresses itself, not without hesitation and doubt, in my giving all royalties from this book to Oxfam and other agencies that work to relieve human suffering.

3. An Introduction to Middle Way Emptiness

UNDOUBTEDLY, THE MOST PROFOUND and surprising feature of quantum mechanics is the principle of nonlocality—that objects cannot be confined to limited regions of space and time and that their connections to the rest of the universe are more important than their isolated existence. The next chapter will make these ideas much more precise. We will also see that they are features of nature that any successor to quantum theory must embody. In other words, nonlocality is a deep truth about the universe that any future replacement for the theory must embody, not just some bizarre feature of today's quantum theory.

With equal certainty, the most fundamental philosophic view within Tibetan Buddhism is the Middle Way view of emptiness. It too is both profound and surprising that objects appear one way but actually exist in a very different way. Perhaps what is most startling is that nonlocality and Middle Way emptiness deeply concur on the nature of reality, not just in broad outline, but in the details. As I discussed in chapter 1, physics and Buddhism have both similarities and significant differences. Nevertheless, no other major religious worldview has such an arresting and detailed connection to modern physics. This has not been fully appreciated nor have the opportunities this connection provides for deepening our understanding of both Buddhism and physics been adequately explored.

As we will see in the next chapter, the detailed connections between emptiness and quantum theory can be presented without any technical background in either Buddhism or physics. The actual reasoning establishing quantum nonlocality can be carefully presented with only simple counting arguments. If you can balance your checkbook, you can follow the reasoning. Likewise in Middle Way emptiness, the difficulties in presenting the ideas are not technical in nature. The problems come because these ideas require a revolution in our understanding of the nature of reality, of how the world actually exists. We never give up old, erroneous, but strongly held views gracefully.

To prepare the ground for the discussion of the relationship between emptiness and quantum nonlocality, this chapter reviews the Middle Way doctrine of emptiness. While there is a vast literature on this subject of which my knowledge is limited, this chapter does present the essential features of Middle Way emptiness.[1] The following chapter then presents a special version of the famous Bell's Inequality, whose experimental violation in a number of elegant experiments firmly establishes quantum nonlocality. Let's begin the discussion of emptiness in my backyard.

Independent Existence and Its Refutation

While writing this chapter, I put a pressure-treated wooden post into the ground outside my home office window. It is part of a dog run for Daisy, my intelligent and rambunctious yellow Labrador retriever. When some potentially tasty morsel, such as a wandering woodchuck, excites Daisy, she can pull mightily on that post. I therefore buried its bottom three feet in concrete. (See figure 3.1.)

As I gaze out my office window, that post seems about as substantial and real as things get. It seems to exist independently of my knowing of it and of Daisy's pulls on it. Without much thought about it, the post seems to exist "from its own side," as the Middle Way says. That expression means that an object's existence does not depend upon things outside itself or upon anybody's knowing or interacting with it. Alternatively, the Middle Way would say that the post appears "findable upon analysis," which means that, if we examine it more closely, its independent nature will shine through more clearly. In short, we instinctively believe that the post inherently or independently exists.

It is important to be clear about how we normally view objects—whether posts or our own personality. If we are not clear about this point—that objects appear to exist from their own side, are findable upon analysis, or that they independently exist—we will never get the proper understanding of emptiness. Because this point is so critical, let us consider another example.

I take a break from working at the computer and go to the kitchen for a drink of water. On the windowsill above the sink is a polished stone, given to my wife as a gift, shown in figure 3.2. This beautifully colored, weighty stone feels very satisfying in my hand. Everybody who handles it loves that smooth, solid weight, which nestles so well in the palm. If anything exists from its own side, this beautiful stone does. If anything exists independently of my knowing or interacting with it, it must be this stone. It does not seem to need the windowsill, kitchen sink, or anything else to exist in a self-contained and integral way. Before it was given to my wife and well after we have died, that stone will exist in its own independent way. You do not have to do any fancy analysis or strain to find it when it rests comfortably and solidly in your hand. Clearly, it independently or inherently exists.

FIGURE 3.1.
Does this post inherently exist?

FIGURE 3.2.
Is this an inherently existent stone?

It is important to define with care what emptiness denies. If we too broadly define inherent or independent existence, nihilism follows—then nothing exists. On the other hand, if we too narrowly define it, substantialism results—then persons and objects have a substantial, immutable nature, something vigorously denied by our everyday experience and the Buddhist principle of impermanence. We therefore must carefully avoid these extremes that the Middle Way considers philosophic crimes. The Middle Way is not a blending of the two extremes but a thoroughgoing refutation of both.

Middle Way Buddhists claim that fully assimilating the doctrine of emptiness frees us from the suffering of *samsara*, the beginningless and inevitable round of birth, aging, suffering, and death. The exalted condition of a buddha, a fully enlightened one, means that we transcend all pairs of opposites: then, *samsara* and *nirvana* are not different. Fully assimilating emptiness transforms us from self-centered individuals shrouded in ignorance to completely enlightened buddhas, embodiments of wisdom and compassion.

The Middle Way spends an enormous amount of philosophic effort showing that our instinctive belief in independent existence is wrong, that there is no such independent or inherent existence to posts, stones, or people. Just to give a flavor of how they establish this pivotal piece of Tibetan Buddhism, I briefly summarize the three general forms of their argument.

First, the Middle Way position argues that the post lacks independent existence because it depends upon innumerable causes and conditions. For example, the post depends upon the tree from which it was sawn, the wood preservative injected into it, the concrete in which it sits; the fact that it has not been struck by lightning; its location in my yard, etc. The post does not exist in a vacuum but is deeply related to and dependent upon its prior causes, conditions, and environment.

Similarly, the stone exists in dependence upon ancient geological processes that generated its chemical composition, swirling patterns of color, and texture. Then, the stone was tumbled for days along with other stones and some abrasive materials to make it smooth. A huge number of people and pieces of equipment transported the stone, displayed it in a store, sold it to the gift giver, and so forth. Then a properly functioning sense of touch, musculature, and coordination in the hand and arm are needed for that satisfying feeling the stone gives when in your hand. This stone may seem to exist on its own right, independently of interacting with anything outside itself, but it too required many outside factors to make it the object we experience today.

Second, the post depends upon its parts and the whole of these parts—the wood, its exact shape, color, its concrete base, location, and so forth, along with the collection and relationship of these parts. Yet, the Middle

Way argues that, if we examine any of those parts on its own or the whole collection of them together, we could not find any independently existent post among them. The stone too depends upon its exact chemical composition, the precise shape, beautifully blended colors, and the harmonious way that these all relate. Analysis shows that, if we examine any of these elements that make up the stone or the collection of them together, we cannot find any independently existent or inherently existent stone.

Third, the post's existence is deeply dependent upon our knowing, which always involves conceptual designation or naming, the gathering together of our sense perceptions, memories, associations, and so forth into an object we designate "post." An unknown post, independent of anybody's conceptual designation simply makes no sense. How could we establish the existence of an unknown post? We could perhaps imagine my post's being known only by me, and then I die without letting the post be seen by somebody else. However, by this exercise, we have just known an imaginary post (the one only seen by me), which is again critically dependent upon our constructing it in our imagination and our conceptual designation. Of course, analogous arguments apply to the stone.

How about dinosaurs that walked on that stone before it was polished and long before humans appeared on earth? Are they dependent on knowing? Again, we make imaginative reconstructions of dinosaurs and stones based on various pieces of archeological and geological data and surreptitiously place a person behind a boulder catching glimpses of the ponderous beasts lumbering along a stony path. Positing an object independent of knowing and conceptual designation may sound reasonable, but it is like positing a stick with only one end.

The normal functioning of mind welds the various pieces of a perception, memories, associations, and expectations together and designates or names the resulting composite object as post or stone. None of the parts or the collection of the parts independently exists, but the post or stone still serves to anchor the dog run or please the eye and hand. Objects lacking inherent existence do function, do bring us help or harm. This mental designation or naming is an appropriate function of mind. The difficulty comes because the mind unconsciously invests the objects with the false character of independent or inherent existence. Because of this false imputation or projection of inherent existence, we overvalue the object or flee from it, thereby spinning the wheel of suffering on the false axle of independent existence.

Finally, let us examine what the post would be like if it independently existed. If something independently exists then, by definition, it is not dependent upon anything outside itself for its existence and nature. It is important to understand that this is precisely what independent existence means. Then, independently existent things—whether posts, stones, or people—could not change or evolve, for nothing outside them could affect their essential nature. They are thus unchangeable. (You might pause for a moment to consider this simple but powerful argument.) If the post is unchangeable, then I need not worry about its decaying, being hit by lightning, or being pulled over by Daisy. But, obviously, nothing exists like that.

Independent existence, which we all habitually believe is the foundation for reality, is in fact a hopelessly contradictory idea. An independently existent thing never existed, and it never will. The Middle Way holds that it is essential to identify clearly what is denied (independent existence); otherwise, emptiness is easily misunderstood as claiming that nothing exists. As I will emphasize below, things and persons clearly exist for the Middle Way. The question is exactly how they exist and function.

It is important to appreciate that emptiness applies to all levels of objects and subjects. Thus, all persons are empty of inherent existence, too. It is often easier to appreciate that objects lack independent existence than to deny the independent existence of subjects. As with objects, whether posts or stones, we need to define clearly what subjectivity is being denied, what kind of selfhood or "I" is in question. For that, we need to examine our experience when we are challenged, for then there is a very strong sense of "I." For this subjective case, consider an example I first discussed in my synchronicity book.[2]

Many years ago, I got the strong urge to go canoeing on a nearby lake. I've enjoyed canoeing since my childhood, and the beautiful late spring day seemed to cry out for it. A friend lent me his canoe, and my wife and I were soon paddling along the shoreline enjoying the beauty and peace of nature. We were both extolling the beauties of Seneca Lake and saying how conducive canoeing was to a relaxing and aesthetic appreciation of nature. Suddenly, a water skier was heading straight for us at top speed. It looked as if he were going to slice our canoe in half, but he veered to the side at the last possible moment, thereby completely drenching me and my wife with cold water. Sputtering disbelief, shock, indignation, then rage—all exploded inside me. "That damn kid! If he tries it again,

I'll stand up in the canoe and whack him with the paddle! How could he do that to me . . . *to me*?!"

After a few moments of intense indignation, I began to laugh heartily, marveling at how quickly my feelings changed from nature mystic to Attila the Hun, from the aspiring *bodhisattva* to bloodthirsty monster. I also guiltily recalled how often the Buddhists emphasize the importance of controlling anger. For example, they say, "How are we harmed by our anger or hatred? Buddha has said that hatred decreases or destroys all our collections of virtue and can lead us into the lowest of the hell realms."[3]

However, the main point here is a philosophic one rather than a moral one—although in Buddhism they always closely connect. From the philosophic perspective, the Middle Way Buddhist notes that right at the height of my indignation there was a clear experience of "I"—the one we all firmly believe inherently or independently exists. Certainly, I had no concern for "turning the other cheek" or for the doctrine of universal compassion or any such principles. However, the critical thing in the example is the "I," the all-important "me" believed to exist independently, standing in bold relief in the light of my indignation.

It is easy to be led astray by the anger in my story, but that is not the point. The important thing is that, at times when we are challenged, we can most easily see the powerful sense of "I." Perhaps another simple example will make this clear. Imagine an academic who is wrongly accused of some gross form of plagiarism. His shock and disbelief will quickly turn to indignation. "*I* would never do such a thing! *I* am scrupulously honest about that sort of thing," he might exclaim. Right at the height of his indignation, there is a very strong sense of an "I," one unjustly accused, an honest man, thinking frantically how he can clear his good name.

At the very height of our anger and indignation, whether from water skiers having fun or the unjust accusations of academics, the Middle Way wants us to identify that strong sense of self, the "I" who appears to exist so vividly, the one so offended. We must analyze this subject with care and realize it is empty, completely lacking in inherent existence. Of course, this is relatively easy to do as I sit here writing this in my office but much more difficult to do in the heat of being challenged. Much practice and purification are needed for that.

This "I" that we instinctively believe inherently or independently exists is thoroughly denied in the doctrine of emptiness, which goes well beyond denying this coarse or low level of the ego. That is just the beginning of the Middle Way's no-self doctrine. Middle Way Buddhists claim that *any* identifiable level of subjectivity is empty of independent existence. Tenaciously clinging to the false belief in an independently existing subject or a self is the primary cause of our suffering, of our bondage to *samsara*—the beginningless cycle of birth, death, and rebirth.

How then do things exist—whether posts, stones, or people? The Middle Way affirms that the post surely functions and provides a solid attachment for the dog run: it helps keep Daisy out of mischief. Most importantly, the post exists as deeply dependent and interrelated to all its causes and conditions, whole and parts, and our knowing of it as "post." Ultimately, the post is a conceptual designation, a complex arrangement of dependency relations that completely lacks independent or inherent existence. It, like all objects and subjects in the universe, is empty of inherent existence, without an independent existence, lacking any self-sufficient essence. It has no essential self-nature and so is continuously transforming, changing, and evolving as it interacts with its infinite web of defining relationships. Thus, impermanence directly expresses emptiness. In other words, the principle of impermanence, which plays such a pivotal role in both the theory and practice of Buddhism, directly follows from emptiness.

Although we wrongly believe that the post inherently exist, its very lack of independent existence allows it to function, to serve as an anchor for a dog run, and to evolve continuously. As discussed above, if the post inherently existed, it would be frozen in its permanence and inability to connect with the environment. Subjectively, my very lack of independent existence allows me to be an empirical individual, a functional person in the world with an identity and love of canoeing. More importantly, my emptiness allows for this naïve person attempting to embody kindness, to evolve into a buddha, a being of infinite wisdom and compassion. Thus, although we often feel that emptiness denies our most precious sense of self, in fact, our lack of inherent existence is the foundation for our spiritual and psychological transformation from darkness into light.

It is important to note that emptiness is a pure negation. It does not replace the false category of inherent existence with some other principle. It just asserts the dependent nature of all phenomena or their emptiness of inherent existence. The Middle Way calls emptiness a "*nonaffirming negation*." To understand that term, consider the case where there are no persons with ambiguous gender. Then I say, "The driver of that car is not a man." That is an affirming negation because it actually asserts that the driver is a woman. So appreciating that emptiness is a nonaffirming negation emphasizes that no new principle is posited to replace the false attribute of independent existence.

Rather than the pure negation of emptiness, we can positively characterize ultimate truth by saying that all things are dependently arisen—dependent upon causes and conditions, whole and parts, and mental designation. Dependent arising emphasizes the deeply relational and interdependent nature of all persons and things and is equivalent to emptiness. Emptiness and dependent arising are like two sides of one hand, with impermanence radiating from both sides.

Projecting Falsehood as the Foundation for Suffering

It is natural at this point to ask the following question: if all subjects and objects truly lack independent existence or are dependently arisen, how is it that they appear to exist independently? The answer is that this false attribute of inherent existence, this incoherent quality that never was and never will be, is projected into or upon subjects and objects. In other words, we *unconsciously* attribute, impute, or assign the false attribute of inherent existence to subjects and objects, people and posts. This projection hangs upon no hook—there is nothing in the object that independently exists.

In later chapters, several examples in physics reveal how the mind unconsciously projects inherent or independent existence into objects. Fortunately, modern physics emphatically shows that nature does not support these projections. We thus have an opportunity to see clearly how the mind projects this false quality into objects that are empty of independent existence.

Psychologists have shown in detail how our psychological projections cause innumerable problems in our interpersonal relations. These projections obscure our perception of the other person, cause us to overvalue or undervalue the person upon whom we project, and inhibit us from seeing our true nature. In a completely analogous way, the philosophic projection of inherent existence obscures the true nature of people and things, forms the false basis for our attachments, obscures our true nature, and is the chief cause of our suffering. This false belief in inherent existence, which we project upon the subject or object, is the major impediment to our enlightenment.

The late Lama Yeshe in his essay "How Delusions Arise" discusses how attachments are rooted in the projection of inherent existence:

> Seeing some kind of desirable object, then, always involves an overestimation. Its good aspects are emphasized so much that you lose all judgment about it. Simultaneously, you view that object as if it were somehow self-existent. You conceive of it as something permanent, existing self-sufficiently the way it appears to you. You fail to see that the way it appears is actually a function of your own projections. Instead, you think that these exaggerated qualities come from the object itself rather than being what you have put onto the object from you own side. You do not see what has happened. This deluded projection covering the object is much thicker than makeup. Impermanent things are viewed as permanent. Objects being in the nature of suffering are thought of as the causes of happiness. And although all things lack true, independent self-existence, they are conceived of as having such self-existence.[4]

Let me give a simple but useful analogy of this process of projecting independent existence or of applying makeup by way of a little story. A theoretical physicist is walking in the woods one day. The giant trees are swaying in the breeze. Changing patterns of sunlight dance across the forest floor. The beauty and majesty of it all overcomes him. He thinks to himself, "How amazing that all of this comes out of a condition in the early big bang when the four forces of nature were unified. The universe cools, the four forces differentiate, galaxies form, planets evolve, and this extraordinarily beautiful woods develops." In the midst of these pleasant reflections, he hears a great crashing in the brush behind him and turns to find a huge grizzly bear charging upon him. He turns and runs in panic. His heart is pounding, the bear is gaining on him, and he can even smell the bear's bad breath. As the bear closes in on him, he trips on a root of one of those majestic trees. Falling to the ground, he cries out, "Oh God!"

Suddenly the scene freezes. A profound stillness pervades everything, and a deep resonant voice booms from the sky and says, "So, when you're in trouble you cry out to me and want my help just like the good Christians who pray fervently to me everyday. But when you're lecturing at the universities, you deny my existence, telling people it's all an expression of the four forces in nature." The physicist, who has been well trained in the importance of logical consistency, replies, "Yes, I admit that would be inconsistent. But how about making the bear more like a good Christian?" God briefly considers this idea and says, "Yes, I can do that."

Suddenly, the stillness and the great voice vanish. The grizzly bear stands upon his hind legs, bows deeply before the physicist, puts its forepaws together in front of his chest and says, "We give thanks for these gifts we are about to receive." He then extends his claws, opens his huge maw, and devours the fallen man.

Our theoretical physicist wakes up from this terrible nightmare screaming in a cold sweat. Set aside any psychological interpretations of the dream and just consider the nature of the various parts of the dream. Upon waking, even though still bathed in terror, the physicist says, "Oh, thankfully, it's only a dream." He acknowledges that it was only a creation of his dreaming mind. All the objects and the dream ego are just constructions in thought.

However, *while in the dream*, it is all as real as any waking experience. Each object from tree to bear appears to exist independently or inherently, to exist from its own side. Therefore, the mind, along with forming the varied objects and subjects in the dream, projects independent self-existence into them. In the dream, the man is fully convinced of the inherent or independent existence of the bear. Its evil-looking fangs and extended claws surely exist from their own side and are findable upon analysis—but who has time for analysis when you're running for your life? The dreamer has no doubt about the independent reality of his terror and his desire to escape. Thus, the dreaming mind projects inherent existence into its own creations, including the terrified physicist who suffers because of it.

In the same way, the waking mind projects independent existence into our sense of self and the objects surrounding it—into all the conceptually designated subjects and objects. This projection is then the false foundation for our attachments and the suffering that follows from them. I am not saying that life is a dream, but that the same projective mechanism, the same unconscious investing of the objects and subjects with inherent existence that gives dreams their vivid reality, is also operative in waking consciousness. Upon this false projection of independent existence, we generate our cravings, aversions, and attachments—the roots of suffering.

For example, I love my family and can think of nothing worse than their being sick, injured, or dying. I intellectually grant that they are empty, just as I am, and that I am projecting inherent existence into them. Nevertheless, despite my intellectual knowledge, emotionally I do not want to accept the impermanence that flows directly from our emptiness. Although I am aware of projecting, I am not able to stop the process. Unfortunately, much suffering follows from my projecting of inherent existence and the consequent failure truly to grasp emptiness and the resulting impermanence. Of course, this is not just my personal problem. We all want to deny our impermanence. We do not even want to show any signs of aging. (Sorry, this chapter must end soon, so I will be on time for my face-lift appointment!)

All this is understandable, but such attachment—whether to posts, unwrinkled skin, or our lives, all of which are naturally impermanent—guarantees suffering. The false projection of inherent existence into objects or person, whether environmental disasters, terrorists, or hated political figures, causes us to flee from or fear these things or people. Whether we are attracted to persons and objects or repelled by them, our projection of inherent existence is the foundation for suffering. In other words, our inability to appreciate emptiness leads inexorably to suffering.

Lama Yeshe gives more details about how projection (both philosophic and psychological) is at the root of suffering. I insert a few explanatory comments in square brackets in the following quotation from his essay "Searching for the Causes of Unhappiness." The italics are in the original.

> Let us look deeper into the nature of feelings. Whether they are happy, unhappy, or neutral, most feelings arise from wrong discriminations. Such discriminations are mistaken because they are based on false projections [of inherent existence] of the mind, which keep you from perceiving the true nature of reality [as empty]. This [projection] can refer to the reality of any phenomenon, outer or inner, animate or inanimate. Feelings do not only arise when one human reacts with another. They can occur in relation to anything. In most

> instances of conflict, there is an object and your disturbed feelings about it are the subject. These may be thought of as distinct and separate from one another—as when one feels, *I hate that person*—but in fact your feeling has somehow created this object. By this I mean that the object of your feeling has nothing whatsoever to do with the reality of any external phenomenon [which we falsely believe independently exists]. It is merely the painted projection of a falsely discriminating mind.
>
> . . . Investigate your mental attitude toward things and discover how you impose your mistaken projections on to the people you meet [psychological projection] and onto all other phenomena as well [philosophic projection].
>
> . . . You will see that your painted sensory world is but the product of mistaken projections and that the feelings aroused by such a fictitious universe keep you shuttling back and forth between elation and despair. This circle of dissatisfaction, built on illusion [the projection of inherent existence], is *samsara* [the wheel of suffering] itself and your investigation will show you that it is fashioned within your own mind.[5]

The structure of suffering is thus deeply rooted in projection. The logical order of the process goes like this. First, there is the projection of inherent or independent existence on phenomena, whether persons or things, our own ego or possessions. Second, this false sense of inherent existence and the accompanying inability to appreciate the fundamental emptiness of all phenomena then provide the fraudulent foundation for the overvaluing of positive or negative objects or persons, what Lama Yeshe calls "feelings." This is how the wheel of *samsara* turns. Of course, we do not experience these steps as a temporal sequence. Rather, the process is the logical sequence of projection of inherent existence → attraction and repulsion → the suffering of *samsara*.

Once we understand emptiness, this projection of the falsehood of inherent existence, and the suffering it causes, we have an innate desire to stop the process. Because we all desire happiness and freedom from suffering, we naturally seek to break the cyclic chain of *samsara*, break out of the realm of suffering. Furthermore, once we understand how it works in ourselves, we can see it work in others and very naturally a strong sense of compassion arises for all those suffering like ourselves from this process of projecting independent existence. In this way, our personal experience gets universalized and emptiness gives rise to compassion. In other words, deep knowledge of reality gives rise to universal compassion. Geshe Kensure Lekden stated it beautifully:

> Just as by understanding emptiness one realizes that it is possible to eradicate cyclic existence and one thereby develops a firm decision to leave cyclic existence, so when one understands that others' suffering is also induced by the misconception of ignorance, one realizes that it is possible to eradicate all suffering and thereby develops a firm decision to free them from misery. Compassion is then a realistic expression of deep knowledge.[6]

Of course, in the Middle Way, the wisdom of emptiness combines with the practice of compassion to generate a buddha, the pinnacle of human development. Once again, we see how knowledge or truth (emptiness) leads to compassion or love.

In the next chapter's discussion of quantum nonlocality, we will see a beautiful example of how the mind unconsciously projects independent existence into nature. Even better, we will see how both theory and experiment converge to show the error in this projection. In other words, physics gives us a unique opportunity to see how we project independent existence into nature and how a careful analysis shows that nature refuses to wear the "makeup" or "paint," as Lama Yeshe calls it.

So far, I have presented the standard view of how our unconscious philosophic projection of inherent existence provides the false foundation for our overvaluing objects and the suffering this process always entails. Here is another dimension of the process. I look out my window and see the extraordinary wildflowers that we planted early this spring. The poppies are a brilliant, deep red. The bachelor buttons are a radiant blue. I know the flowers will soon fade and that, in a few years, the grasses and weeds will take over the wildflower bed. This doesn't make me sad. I'm also looking forward to eating a delicious lunch with garden vegetables on my back porch. I know that I'll soon be hungry again, that my satisfaction is short-lived, just as with the ephemeral beauty of the flowers. However, none of this lack of permanence makes me sad or frustrated.

With a little deeper reflection, I realize that what I'm really after is the *permanent satisfaction of desires*. I don't mind the flowers fading as long as I can see them again. I don't mind getting hungry again as long as I can look forward to supper. However, if you told me I could never see the flowers again nor eat fresh salad, I would be exceedingly depressed. Pleasant experiences can come and go with little sadness—as long as I can permanently remain as their enjoyer. In short, I am clinging to the permanent satisfaction of my desires, to my own ego as the enduring enjoyer. I know intellectually that my ego is impermanent, that my eyesight is fading and will get weaker, that my appetite will one day cease. Nevertheless, I cannot stop my desire for the continuation of enjoyments, the result of my unconsciously projecting independent existence into my ego and the false promise of permanence that such projection creates.

The Prison of Ego

This false foundation generated by the projection of independent existence and our continuous effort to sustain and feed our egos as permanent enjoyers is the foundation for our selfishness and fear of death. We will do anything to maintain our ego's existence, including heroic, ruinously expensive, and painful medical procedures. We thereby put ourselves and our needs first and find the practice of compassion very difficult. Truly, we are prisoners of the ego, of our false belief in our own permanent existence as enjoyers, in our own precious selves.

If we carefully examine our experience, we realize what an enormous amount of energy goes into propping up our false sense of self. Not only am I indignant when splashed with cold water, not only do I want permanently to enjoy the satisfaction of desires, I am constantly trying to affirm my ego, proving to myself and others just how important, talented, and heavenly I am. Of course, this is not unique to me. We are all trying to be "somebody," persons of real significance and worth. This "somebody complex" is not just a harmless part of the human condition but the "bars" that keep us locked into the prison of self. Every disappointment, every defeat, is a blow to our lovingly held sense of self and another dose of suffering. Every time our desires are not met or we feel slighted or not properly recognized, we add to our sentence in the prison of self. On the other hand, every victory or sense of personal accomplishment solidifies our false sense of self, and we again add to our sentence in the ego's prison.

Not only does this prison cause us much suffering, it also blinds us to the needs of others and puts our desires before all else. It is always all about our individual happiness and satisfaction. The needs of others come in a very distant second. Trapped in our narcissism, we are self-absorbed and cannot be genuinely concerned for other people. Such selfishness is the most profound cause of our inability to act compassionately, to be genuinely concerned with the welfare of others. Therefore, in the prison of self, we are all in solitary confinement, entombed in our own self-centeredness.

The saddest result of all this is that the very thing that every person desires above all else—his or her own lasting happiness—is only achieved by breaking out of this prison and being genuinely concerned for the welfare of others. As the Dalai Lama says, practicing compassion is in our own enlightened self-interest:

> Each of us has responsibility for all humankind. It is time for us to think of other people as true brothers and sisters and to be concerned with their welfare, with lessening their suffering. Even if you cannot sacrifice your own benefit entirely, you should not forget the concerns of others. We should think more about the future and benefit of all humanity.
>
> Also, if you try to subdue your selfish motives—anger and so forth—and develop more kindness and compassion for others, ultimately you yourself will benefit more than you would otherwise. So sometimes I say that the wise selfish person should practice this way. Foolish selfish people are always thinking of themselves, and the result is negative. Wise selfish people think of others, help others as much as they can, and the result is that they too receive benefit.
>
> This is my simple religion. There is no need for temples; no need for complicated philosophy. Our own brain, our own heart is our temple; the philosophy is kindness.[7]

Just as in the psychological case, a mere recognition of the projection of independent existence, with all the suffering for ourselves and others that it entails, is not enough to stop the projection. In other words, we can know that we are in the prison of self and even understand how we got there and how much suffering it generates, yet a break-out is not easy.

This jailbreak is going to take much effort, perhaps lifetimes of study, moral re-education, and meditation.

Rather than end this chapter on such a somber note, let me turn to the *bodhisattva* vow that the Dalai Lama loves so deeply. There Shantideva says, "For as long as space endures . . . may I too abide to dispel the misery of the world." Within the Middle Way, space is a permanent principle because it is defined as the "lack of obstructive contact," the ability to accommodate objects. By its very definition, space has always lacked obstructive contact, and thus there always has been and always will be space. Therefore, we can take comfort that, despite our inveterate projection of independent existence and all the suffering that follows from it, there are also compassionate beings who work permanently to "dispel the misery."

4. The Physics of Peace

Quantum Nonlocality and Emptiness

Introduction

It is difficult to think of physics and peace at the same time. We usually think of physics as a way to amplify our violence through the production of weapons. However, there is an even more important role for physics since it contributes mightily to our worldview, our comprehensive interpretation of the universe and of ourselves and how the two relate.

Unfortunately, our modern worldview is still far too influenced by classical physics, the view of Sir Isaac Newton and his followers. Newton envisioned the universe as being built from independently or inherently existent point particles, entities existing in their own right that secondarily come together to build more complex structures from galaxies to people. Figure 4.1 illustrates the classical view of entities, whether particles or people. There the entities are substantial things with the solidity of iron posts. Relations to other objects (other posts) are through dashed lines since they are less real and substantial than the posts they

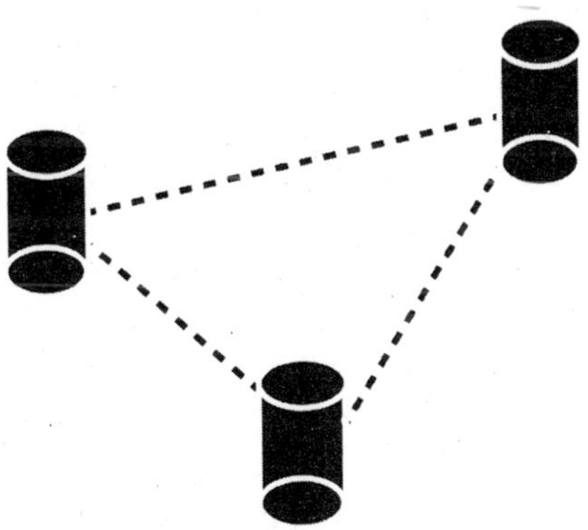

FIGURE 4.1. *Classical posts*

connect. If classical particles could talk, they would say something like, "My independent reality is primary. My relationships to other objects are secondary."

Given its fundamental importance, the quantum mechanical view of entities is much less influential in shaping our modern worldview than it should be. In the last two decades, we have come to understand that the relationships between quantum entities are often more important, more real, than the isolated existence of the entities. Many philosophers of science consider this view, which comes from studies of quantum nonlocality, to be the most significant finding since the birth of science. In this chapter, I explain exactly what quantum nonlocality is and discuss its intimate connection to Middle Way emptiness. Through this connection, the implications of quantum nonlocality and its connection to peace become much deeper and richer.

Figure 4.2 illustrates the quantum mechanical view. Now the objects are diagrammed with dashed lines with solid connecting lines. This illustrates the idea that the relationships are more fundamental, more real, than any isolated objects. Actually, an object's existence depends upon its relationship to other objects. If the quantum particles could speak

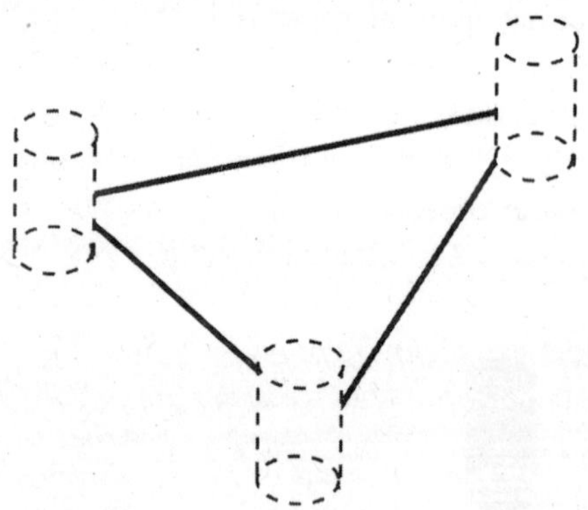

FIGURE 4.2. *Quantum posts*

they would say, "I exist in a well-defined way because of my relationship to other particles. I have no independent existence." Such a view, which has taken much hard labor to substantiate, has not been assimilated into collective culture. It obviously has enormous implications for both personal and world peace.

Physicists rarely discuss how physics shapes our worldview and influences our culture. A notable exception is the late David Bohm, internationally known for his important work at the foundations of quantum mechanics. Bohm writes:

> It is proposed that the widespread and pervasive distinctions between people (race, nation, family, profession, etc., etc.), which are now preventing mankind from working together for the common good, and indeed, even for survival, have one of the key factors of their origin in a kind of thought that treats things as inherently divided, disconnected, and "broken up" into yet smaller constituent parts. Each part is considered to be essentially independent and self-existent.[1]

Here I will show in detail how the quantum view differs from the belief of classical physics that "[e]ach part is considered to be essentially independent and self-existent." We instead have a mysterious level of interconnectedness that is more profoundly related than we can conceive using any models from classical physics.

A standard tenet within the Middle Way says that emptiness itself is empty, without independent essence. I have not seen it said anywhere, but this must imply that the Middle Way's relationship to other traditions defines it at the deepest level. In other words, emptiness implies that the Middle Way is defined by how it relates to other worldviews. Thus, comparative philosophy is built into the foundation of the Middle Way. In our day, so dominated by science, the Middle Way should be examined in relation to modern science. Therefore, along with my personal need to weave my inner and outer worlds into a harmonious fabric, a comparative study of the Middle Way with physics expresses the Middle Way's deepest reality as relational, as empty of independent existence.

The most penetrating understanding of quantum nonlocality comes from the celebrated experimental violation of Bell's Inequalities. Although much debate surrounds the proper interpretation of quantum mechanics, we can avoid this controversy by focusing on these inequalities, which have extensive experimental and theoretical support.[2] As I will show, this analysis is independent of the present formulation of quantum mechanics. Therefore, any future replacement for quantum mechanics must embody nonlocality. Happily, we can show all this without requiring any technical background in physics or mathematics. Only a little reasoning and counting are necessary.

There is no attempt here to "prove" the doctrine of emptiness by showing its expression at the deepest level of modern physics. That would imply that physics is the more profound view and that we are using it to deduce the lesser reality, the Middle Way. Instead, I like to think of it is a conversation between two very different traditions, which are most fundamentally defined by their dialogue, by their mutually dependency.

For me, the dialogue began nearly forty years ago when I was a graduate student at Cornell University. Then I looked up Einstein's major challenge to the conceptual foundations of quantum mechanics in Einstein, Podolsky, and Rosen (EPR).[3] After all these years, I still vividly recall the dark green bindings of the *Physical Review*, where I was in the library, and most importantly, how the edges of the pages were blackened by the countless fingers that had turned them. I had never seen a physics journal with such obvious marks of wear. Why did so many find EPR so compelling? In answering this question, we can begin to understand how the most fundamental insight into the nature of physical reality since Galileo connects to peace, both personal and global.

The Challenge of EPR

Although Einstein's work laid many of the foundation stones for quantum mechanics, he was never happy with the theory. From the late 1920s up to 1935 when EPR was published, he engaged in a number of debates with Niels Bohr and others on the conceptual foundations of quantum mechanics.[4] Many physicists consider these debates to be the most thrilling and important discussions in science, on a par with the debate that raged around Galileo over the structure of the solar system. To appreciate this clash of titans, we first review the idea of complementarity, the very heart of quantum mechanics.

For a visual analog of complementarity, let your eyes relax and stare at figure 4.3 opposite. You will see that there are two competing views of the square. At first, one surface appears closer to you. After looking for a moment, a different surface will appear closer to you. Upon further looking, those two views alternate but never appear simultaneously. Here is a simple example of complementarity. The two views are equally real and important, but they are mutually exclusive.

There are three important points about complementarity. First, complementary properties (such as waves and particles) require mutually

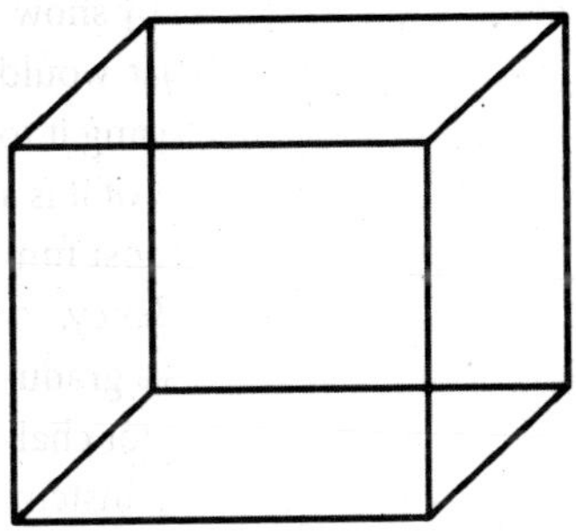

FIGURE 4.3. *Complementarity*

exclusive experimental conditions for their study. To study the wave nature of a quantum system requires an arrangement of the laboratory apparatus that rules out a simultaneous study of its particle properties. These mutually exclusive experimental conditions prevent any conflict or inconsistency between the disparate properties. Second, both poles of a complementary pair are equally real and important in characterizing a quantum system. This eliminates any reductive strategy for understanding complementary properties. For example, you cannot say that a particle is merely a tightly localized wave. Third, a unitary reality encompasses all complementary properties in the form of *possibilities* for manifestation—discussed in more detail below. This unitary reality has an abstract mathematical expression in the wave function and the equations governing its evolution. The unitary reality is not on the level of the complementary properties that it unifies nor does it obliterate their differences.

Although there are innumerable pairs of complementary properties in quantum mechanics, I focus on the well-known complementarity between waves and particles. In any quantum mechanical system, we can choose to study its wave nature or its particle nature; but since they require mutually exclusive experimental arrangements for their study, we can never simultaneously display both wave and particle properties. I call the "realist temptation" the view that, although we cannot study the wave nature of an electron when we are examining its particle nature, the wave nature still exists in a well-defined way. In other words, we want to believe that the electron has intrinsic properties that are independent of the experimental situation. Conversely, when we study the wave nature, then the particle nature still independently exists but is just not observable. In Buddhist language, it has inherent or independent existence. As we will see, this is *not* the case, and we are projecting this independent existence into nature at the deepest levels. We are providing the false "makeup" as Lama Yeshe told us toward the end of the previous chapter.

The realist temptation is a natural expectation based on everyday experience of conventional reality. However, as we will see, our experience with conventional reality, the world of stones, posts, and flowers, often leads us astray when considering the fundamental structure of nature. Instead, quantum mechanics tells us, "Do not succumb to the realist temptation; revealing one member of a complementary pair means that the other does not exist in a well-defined way." It is not just that the members of a complementary pair require mutually exclusive experimental conditions; the unmanifest one does not exist in any reasonable sense of the word. It certainly does not inherently exist.

Einstein found this a troubling aspect of quantum mechanics and in EPR sought to show that nature was not truly this way and, therefore, that the quantum mechanical description was incomplete. To get to the essence of EPR's scheme to show the incompleteness of quantum mechanics, we need to understand the notion of correlation. Physicists often speak about making measurements on widely separated correlated particles, those sharing similar properties. Here is a macroscopic example. Consider my pair of gloves. Let's say a friend visits my home, mistakenly picks up one of my gloves, and carries it back to his home. Once I realized what has happened, all I need to do is see whether I have the left- or right-handed glove to know which glove my friend has. If, for example, I have the left-handed glove, then my friend clearly has the right-handed glove. We know this because the gloves are correlated pairs: one right- and one left-handed. Of course, this correlation is independent of the distance between the gloves.

There are several big differences between what EPR discussed and my gloves. First, each of the correlated particles in EPR has a complementary nature, in that each member of the pair can exhibit both wave and particle properties. (That would be something like each glove of the pair being able to exhibit right- or left-handedness, depending upon exactly how we observed it. Although that might sometimes be convenient, it is hardly the nature of gloves!) Second, as we will see, the kind of correlations found between particles in EPR-type experiments seem to involve some mysterious, faster-than-light action at a distance. However, we need to understand EPR before we can get to that mystery. Third, the correlations are statistical, as most quantum phenomena are. They are not perfect correlations but hold a certain well-defined percentage of the time.

EPR state an important definition: "*If without in any way disturbing a system we can predict with certainty the value of a physical quantity, then there exists an element of physical reality corresponding to this physical quantity.*" (This definition might seem harmless enough, but it actually asserts the independent existence of the physical quantity that we can predict with certainty without disturbing the system. So we are right in the thick of a fundamental debate!) EPR then consider a pair of correlated particles, one moving off to the left, and the other to the right. Consider the case when we measure the position of the particle on the left; then, since the particles are correlated, we can predict with certainty the position of the particle on the right without disturbing that particle in any way.

The typical way of ensuring that a measurement on the left does not affect the particle on the right is to separate the particles such that no information can travel between them during the time between any measurements on them. (Keep in mind that, according to the *principle of locality*, no information or energy can travel faster than the speed of light.) For example, let's say that the particles are one light minute apart (the distance between the sun and earth is eight light minutes), and we make measurements on the left and right particles that are only seconds apart. Here we are ensuring no disturbance of one particle measurement on the other by the principle of locality—no information transfers faster than the speed of light.

Since the idea of locality is so important, another example is in order. Imagine that we have pairs of unscrupulous twins taking exams. Because they are clever swindlers, we want to be sure that they cannot cheat, that they can have no influence on each other. The only way we can truly guarantee no cheating is to separate them widely and carefully time the exams. For example, imagine that the exam takes one minute to complete, and we put one twin on Mars and one on Earth. Each twin takes the exam at exactly the same time. Since they are about twenty light minutes apart, their exams are taken at the same time, and the exams take one minute, there is no way that one twin can communicate with the other for the purposes of cheating.

Return to EPR's experiment when we measure the position of the particle on the left. By appropriate separations and measurement timings, we can be sure that there is no disturbance between the particles. Then, because of the correlation between the particles, the position of the right particle is, according to EPR's definition, an "element of reality." However, we could equally well have measured the wave properties of the left particle. Because they are correlated, we can then predict with certainty and without any disturbance the wave properties of the right particle. Therefore, the particle on the right must have two elements of reality: both particle and wave properties. However, this is contrary to complementarity, which says that no particle can simultaneously have both wave and particle properties. This led EPR to believe that quantum mechanics does not give a full description of reality and is therefore incomplete.

In a subsequent issue of the *Physical Review*, Niels Bohr responded to the serious challenge posed by EPR.[5] As his assistant said, "The onslaught came down upon us as a bolt form the blue. Its effect on Bohr was remarkable. . . . When one realizes the fundamental nature of the issues at stake, it becomes easier to understand the state of exaltation in which Bohr accomplished this work."[6] It is difficult to imagine how a simple argument could cause such an enormous explosion at the foundations of quantum mechanics—one still reverberating more than seventy years later, as hot debate about the conceptual foundations of quantum mechanics and the blackened edges of EPR show. However, complementarity is an expression of the deepest mathematical structures within quantum mechanics. There can be no modifications of that idea without major revisions to the entire theory, both mathematically and conceptually.

In his reply, where the italics are Bohr's and the insertions in square brackets are mine, Bohr states that EPR

> contains an inherent ambiguity as regards the meaning of the expression "without in any way disturbing a system." Of course, [because of locality] there is in a case like that just considered no question of a mechanical disturbance of the system under investigation during the last critical stage of the measuring procedure. But even at this state there is essentially the question of *an influence on the very* [experimental] *conditions which define the possible types of predictions regarding the future behaviour of the system.* Since these conditions constitute an inherent element of the description of any phenomenon to which the term "physical reality" can be properly attached, we

> see that the argumentation of the mentioned authors does not justify their conclusions that quantum-mechanical description is essentially incomplete.[7]

If you find Bohr's statement baffling, you are in good company. It is a very subtle point in quantum mechanics. He is saying that you can never disregard the experimental conditions that define the possible types of measurements you can make, even when you do not actually make them. In other words, you cannot consider quantum properties independent of the total experimental arrangement.

"Discussion with Einstein on Epistemological Problems in Atomic Physics" is Bohr's best essay on his breathtaking debates with Einstein, written more than thirty years after EPR. There Bohr writes:

> We have here to do with a typical example of how the complementary phenomena appear under mutually exclusive experimental arrangements and are just faced with the impossibility, in the analysis of quantum effects, of drawing any sharp separation between an independent behaviour of atomic objects and their interactions with the measuring instruments which serve to define the conditions under which the phenomena occur.[8]

At this point, Bohr stresses the impossibility of treating quantum properties independent of the entire measurement situation that defines what phenomena can occur. From a Buddhist perspective, we would say that he is explicitly denying inherent or independent existence to quantum properties. He is stressing how quantum properties are only defined within the context of the entire experimental setup. They lack independent existence and the very properties we can consider are dependent upon the precise configuration of the experimental apparatus.

Despite the decades-long running disagreements between Bohr and Einstein on truly fundamental principles, they always had the greatest respect and affection for each other. For example, after their first meeting in April 1920, Einstein wrote Bohr: "Not often in life has a person, by his mere presence, given me such joy as you did. I am now studying your great papers and in so doing—especially when I get stuck somewhere—I have the pleasure of seeing your youthful face before me, smiling and explaining. I have learned much from you, especially also about your attitude regarding scientific matters." Bohr then replied, "To me it was one of the greatest experiences ever to meet and talk with you. I cannot express how grateful I am for all the friendliness with which you met me on my visit to Berlin. You cannot know how great a stimulus it was for me to have the long hoped for opportunity to hear your views on the questions that have occupied me. I shall never forget our talks."[9]

FIGURE 4.4. *Bohr and Einstein*
(Photograph by Paul Ehrenfest, courtesy AIP Emilio Segre Visual Archives)

Knowing how difficult it is for scientists to maintain a friendship while being intellectual antagonists for thirty-five years, it is especially inspiring to read a 1961 interview that Bohr had six years after Einstein's death. With only one year to live, Bohr said, "Einstein was so incredibly sweet. I want also to say that now, several years after Einstein's death, I can still see Einstein's smile before me, a very special simile, both knowing, humane, and friendly."[10]

No person before or since has dominated the development of quantum mechanics as Bohr did. Despite the high regard that the physics community had for him, many were not satisfied with his response to EPR and his general interpretation of quantum mechanics. Einstein and several others were certainly not won over to his side, and the debates simmered in the following decades. EPR's claim of the incompleteness of quantum mechanics inspired many people to work on so-called "hidden variable theories."[11] These alternatives to quantum mechanics attempted to build theories that had complete specifications of the properties of quantum mechanical objects, independent of the experimental arrangement. In other words, they tried to build theories in which quantum objects had intrinsic or inherent natures that are fully specified by the hidden variables.

Quantum mechanics is unprecedented in both the extraordinary scope of its applications and the accuracy of its predictions. It has never failed an experimental test, and an extraordinary array of diverse and elegant experiments confirm its predictions with exquisite accuracy. In terms of scope, accuracy, and mathematical elegance (an important criterion for physicists), it is undoubtedly the best theory in the history of physics. Despite these astounding successes, the interpretation of the theory is still unsettled, and EPR was for a half century the rallying point for the dissenters from Bohr's view. Although there are still battles over many points in quantum mechanics, the issues raised by EPR were resolved fifty years later though a combination of elegant theory and precise measurement now known as the experimental violation of the Bell inequalities. Today there is no doubt that EPR, although a seminal paper, is wrong. Understanding just how this is so will deepen our appreciation of quantum mechanics and also of emptiness.

Nonlocality and the Experimental Violations of Bell's Inequalities

The EPR paper motivated searching examinations of the conceptual foundations of quantum mechanics. In 1964, John Bell[12] building on earlier work by David Bohm[13] reformulated the issue raised by EPR to show clearly the conflict between hidden variable theories and quantum mechanics. Eventually, his inequalities (based, as we will soon see, on the belief in independent existence) were tested in various laboratories and clearly shown to be violated, thereby eliminating the possibility of hidden variable theories. Today, thanks to advances in modern technology, it is now possible to have undergraduate juniors and seniors confirm these predictions in the laboratory, as they do in the quantum mechanics course I teach at Colgate University. We thus know that nature is inherently nonlocal. *Nonlocality* is the inability to localize a system in a given region of space and time. Stated positively, well-studied physical systems show instantaneous interconnections or correlations among their parts—true instantaneous action-at-a-distance.

For example, consider two widely separated regions, A and B. In nonlocal phenomena, what happens in region A instantaneously influences what happens in region B and vice versa. Surprisingly, this instantaneous interaction or dependency occurs without any information or energy exchange between regions A and B. Yet the effects are strong and do not weaken with the distance between regions A and B. The experiments discussed in this section reveal interconnectedness without energy exchanges. This nonlocality goes beyond anything explicable by classical ideas. This is mysterious territory. To paraphrase Niels Bohr, if you study it and do not find it mysterious, then you have not understood it. (Of course, that fact does not absolve me from presenting a coherent discussion of the ideas!)

As we will see, the interconnectedness, nonseparability, nonlocality, or entanglement between parts (all approximate synonyms) is so complete that the point of view of separable parts is less fundamental and less significant than the nonseparable nature of the system. This is what I meant above when I said that, if quantum particles could talk they would say, "I exist in a well-defined way because of my relationship to other particles. I have no independent existence." These are truly revolutionary ideas in physics and philosophy. We have neither fully understood nor assimilated these ideas, but there is no doubt that correlated quantum systems are manifestly nonlocal.

To establish nonlocality rigorously, we need to be certain that regions A and B are truly separated from any possible exchange of information or forces, from any causal interaction. With fast electronics, physicists use the principle of locality to isolate parts of a quantum system in the critical Bell's Inequality experiments, just as we did to ensure no cheating between the unscrupulous twins. Rather than talk about laboratories, let me transplant the experiment to a Tibetan monastery. In that macroscopic realm, we reap the triple benefit of making things easier to understand, crashing headlong into some of our cherished philosophic presuppositions (the projection of inherent existence), and preparing the way for a subsequent comparison between nonlocality and emptiness in Tibetan Buddhism. In what follows, I have refined and expanded an earlier analysis to make it more appropriate for my present goals.[14]

Experiments with Tsongkhapa's Bells

Tsongkhapa is the eminent fourteenth-century Middle Way Buddhist commentator and founder of the Gelukba order of Tibetan Buddhism.

Among the Himalayan lamas of Tibetan Buddhism, he is surely the *Chomolungma* (Mount Everest). In our tale, one day an itinerant bell salesman came to Tsongkhapa's monastery and offered him a bargain on some ritual bells—enough to equip all his monasteries. But he had to buy many bells in one large lot to qualify for the deep discount. Figure 4.5 shows an example of the bells, each of which consists of a pair of resonators suspended from a connecting cord. Striking the resonators together makes an exquisite and long-lasting ring that we can follow inward in meditation and prayer.

FIGURE 4.5. *Tibetan bells*

Although the bells he tried had an enchanting sound, their prices were so low that Tsongkhapa was justifiably suspicious. Many bells were in the best Tibetan Buddhist artistic tradition with all the orthodox iconography, but a significant fraction was of the more primitive Bön variety. Tsongkhapa also noticed that some bells were made from a cheap alloy rather than bronze. Finally, some bells were so poorly constructed that they cracked after several vigorous rings. Given this poor quality control, Tsongkhapa wanted to know about the artistic merit, bronze content, and construction strength of the bells before filling the Gelukba monasteries with them. He could visually examine the bells to learn their artistic merit or melt them down to analyze their bronze content or determine the construction strength of a bell by finding the force required for gross deformation. However, these tests are mutually exclusive in that he could perform only one of them on a given resonator. This follows because the materials test (melting) precludes the construction strength test (gross deformation), while both melting and deforming preclude artistic evaluation.

I intentionally exclude possibilities such as first ascertaining artistic merit and then melting or deforming. With this critical constraint, the tests are complementary in the quantum mechanical sense—we cannot perform them simultaneously on the same resonator since they require mutually exclusive experimental arrangements. They are complementary like the wave and particle attributes of light discussed above. *This complementarity is a significant departure from our normal experience in the macroscopic world, and it is a critical assumption if my macroscopic example is to work.* Such complementarity pervades quantum mechanics, but we almost never encounter it in normal experience.

We might ask, "What is the resonator's strength when I know its bronze content?" Laboratory experiment and quantum theory converge here to tell us that the strength is not well-defined when I know the bronze content. It is not just that we require mutually exclusive experimental procedures to determine the strength (gross deformation) versus the bronze content (melting). That would be only an epistemological limitation—a limitation on our knowing. *The issue is ontological, about its actual being—the system, measured or unmeasured, does not simultaneously possess both well-defined complementary properties.* It is important to appreciate that, in the early days of quantum mechanics, it was believed that the measuring process, no matter how delicate or sophisticated, inevitably disturbed the state of the system. Although this is true, this view suggests the entirely mistaken idea that the system has some well-defined nature independent of measurement, which measurement then disturbs. In fact, we now understand that the system is intrinsically indeterminate prior to measurement. It does not have a well-defined nature that is "disturbed" into the measured value.

As the experimental violation of the Bell inequalities will show, within a well-specified measurement situation—let's say we measure bronze content—we can only consider one of the complementary properties (the bronze content) to have a well-defined value; the others (both artistic and strength) are unspecified and unspecifiable. Of course, EPR tried unsuccessfully to get around this constraint of complementarity.

So let's keep the complementary nature of the artistic style, bronze content, and construction strength in mind and return to Tsongkhapa's bells. Although preliminary testing showed that the resonators always seemed paired (both resonators of a pair always passed or failed the same test), the mutually exclusive nature of the tests frustrated Tsongkhapa's desire to analyze the bells more closely. For example, complementarity prevented him from simultaneously knowing the bronze content and strength of a given resonator. In fact, as stressed above, knowing one precludes the others from having well-defined values. *Nevertheless, let's continue with the natural, but incorrect, assumption that the properties are simultaneously well defined, even if the mutually exclusive experimental conditions prohibit our simultaneously knowing these properties.* (Of course, this is the forbidden realist temptation.) Some hidden variable theories, which are rivals to standard quantum mechanics, also make this assumption. However, recent experiments, such as the one discussed here, have proven them wrong.

What we are doing here is a standard approach in Middle Way philosophic argument. We are disproving the hidden variable theories (an expression of the realist temptation) by first assuming the truth of their assertions and then showing that they lead to inconsistency with reality.

To attempt to circumvent complementarity, the bell salesman suggests the following elegant experiment. From a dispatching room in the center of the monastery, one member of the matched pair of resonators is taken to a testing room on the far left side of the monastery and the other to a testing room on the far right of the monastery. (See figure 4.6, which has a monastery with galactic dimensions in light years!) In the left room, one bell resonator is given either test A (artistic style), B (bronze content), or C (construction strength). Which test to administer is randomly determined, and the tests are all pass or fail. Passing the artistic test means the resonator's style is Tibetan Buddhist, passing the bronze test means it is all bronze, and passing the construction strength test means it is strong. Independently and randomly in the right room, one of the three mutually exclusive pass-fail tests (A, B, or C) is performed on the other matched bell resonator.

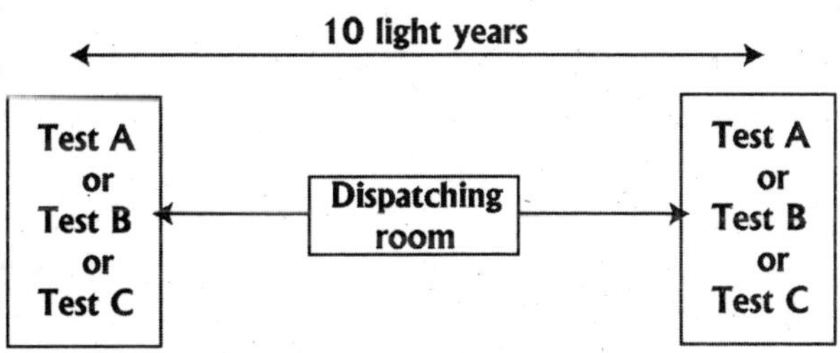

FIGURE 4.6. *Testing Tsongkhapa's bells*

Many in the monastery (including the bell salesman) have occult powers, or *siddhis*; therefore, extreme care has to be taken in the testing procedure. To guard against any cheating or collusion, the fully random and independent selection of tests A, B, or C in the widely separated rooms is done so that no information about test selection or measurement results could propagate between the rooms in time for this information to be useful in any cheating scheme. Physicists of all persuasions use the hallowed locality principle (no energy or information can travel faster than the speed of light) to guarantee that the two sides are completely free from interactions. For example, imagine that the rooms are ten light years apart, the tests require only one second to be performed, and the independent and random test selection occurs simultaneously in each room just one second before the test is given. Therefore, even if a salesman's assistant on the left signaled the test selection or measurement result found there to somebody on the right, this information would take too long to travel the ten light years to be useful for cheating. The locality principle thus precludes information exchange or influences between the sides. The two testing rooms are fully isolated. (Here I assume that locality constrains *siddhis*—it probably does not.)

Because of the complementary nature of the tests, a given pair of resonators can only have two different tests performed on them; for example, test A on the left with B on the right or test C on the left and B on the right. Now with an unlimited supply of bells for the proposed experiment, the monks perform these mutually exclusive pass-fail tests a large number of times and collect the data. I use the following convenient notation: A–B denotes giving test A (artistic style) on the left and test B (bronze content) on the right, while C–B denotes giving test C (construction strength) on the left and B on the right, and so on. The data collected naturally divide into two cases: case 1 when the tests on the left and right happen, through the random test selections, to be the same (A–A, B–B, or C–C), or case 2, when the tests are different (A–B, A–C, B–A, B–C, C–A, or C–B). First, examine case 1 data.

Case 1 Data

When the *tests are the same* on both sides, we find that both resonators always have the same artistic style, bronze content, or construction strength, and it is equally likely that they will both pass or both fail any given test. We never find, for example, that one is bronze and the other alloy or that one is constructed well and the other poorly.

If the resonators are truly matched pairs, we fully expect perfect correlation between the results of tests on both sides revealed in case 1. However, without some theoretical assumptions, case 1 data tells us nothing about what we can expect for case 2, when the tests are different on each side.

Einstein's Interpretation of the Experiment

Here I'll develop an interpretation of the data based on the assumptions that Einstein so eloquently defended. Of course, he never actually made this interpretation since the work described here was done many years after he died. Nonetheless, it is accurate to say that Einstein's lifelong criticism of the conceptual foundations of quantum mechanics was the motivation for much of the Bell inequality analysis. In fact, the idea of separating the correlated systems for testing came from EPR. Einstein's presence hovers over all these discussions about the foundations of quantum mechanics.

Einstein's early written critique of quantum mechanics does not contain his clearest formulation of the philosophic issues. The best statement of his philosophical position is from a 1948 paper in *Dialectica*. The following quotation goes brilliantly to the heart of the matter. It is from the translation and commentary by Donald Howard. Here Einstein develops an idea that later became known as Einstein *separability*.

> If one asks what is the characteristic of the realm of physical ideas independently of the quantum-theory, then above all the following attracts our attention: the concepts of physics refer to a real external world, i.e., ideas are posited of things that claim a "real existence" independent of the perceiving subject (bodies, fields, etc.). . . . [I]t is characteristic of these things that they are conceived of as being arranged in a space-time continuum. Further, it appears to be essential for this arrangement of things introduced in physics that, at a specific time, these things claim an existence independent of one another, in so far as these things "lie in different parts of space." Without

> such an assumption of the mutually independent existence (the "being-thus") of spatially distant things, an assumption which originates in everyday thought, physical thought in the sense familiar to us would not be possible. Nor does one see how physical laws could be formulated and tested without such a clean separation. Field theory [the theory of electromagnetic or gravitational fields, for example] has carried out this principle to the extreme, in that it localizes within infinitely small (four-dimensional) space-elements the elementary things existing independently of one another that it takes as basic, as well as the elementary laws it postulates for them.
>
> For the relative independence of spatially distant things (A and B), this idea is characteristic: an external influence on A has no *immediate effect* on B; this is known as the "principle of local action," which is applied consistently only in field theory.[15]

The principle of local action embodies the idea that the velocity of light is the maximum transmission speed for any information or physical effect. Since light speed is finite, there can be "no *immediate effect*." Bell experiments (both Tsongkhapa's and John Bell's) use the locality principle to isolate each side and prevent any collusion or cheating between test selection or results on the left and right.

More important for our discussion than locality is the "mutually independent existence (the 'being-thus') of spatially distant things, an assumption which originates in everyday thought." Today we call this Einstein separability. Objects separated in space and therefore free of interaction are considered to exist independently, to have intrinsic well-defined properties. It is upon this fundamentally independent existence that relationships are built, but the relationships are considered less real, less fundamental than the "mutually independent existence" of the entities that are related. Einstein firmly believes that it is not possible to do physics without this assumption from daily life.

Let us be clear. Einstein is just formalizing a principle "which originates in everyday thought." We usually believe that, if objects are free of interacting, then they have a mutually independent existence. This is such an obvious truth for Einstein (and most of us) that, if this "being-thus" were absent, then "physical thought in the sense familiar to us would not be possible." In addition to postulating mutually independent existence, Einstein is claiming that things have a "'real existence' independent of the perceiving subject." Thus, for Einstein, objects have two essential properties: first, they have mutually independent existence, and second, they are independent of our knowing. Of course, these two assumptions are precisely the belief in independent or inherent existence, or existence from its own side—exactly what emptiness denies. From a traditional Middle Way point of view, Einstein is doing us an enormous favor by carefully defining the object of negation—inherent or independent existence. The Middle Way always stresses that, without such a careful definition, we can easily misunderstand the principle of emptiness and fall into the evils of either nihilism or eternalism.

Since I have introduced so many terms with both common and technical meanings, it is useful to summarize briefly how the terms are used. I do that in Table 4.1 below.

Term	**Definition**
Locality or the principle of local action	All physical influences travel at speeds less than or equal to the speed of light. [Ensures the isolation of the two sides of the experiment.]
Einstein separability	"Mutually independent existence (the 'being-thus') of spatially distant things." [Inherent existence for Buddhists.]
Nonlocality, nonseparability, entanglement, interdependence, interconnectedness (all used synonymously here)	The violation of Einstein separability or mutually independent existence. According to locality, events in region A are spatially separate from those in region B, yet strong, instantaneous correlations connect events in A to those in B. Yet, no information or forces connect the regions.

TABLE 4.1. *Definition of terms*

This Bell analysis has been generalized to deal with the complication of theories that only assume probabilities rather than definite values for properties. I have dealt with that elsewhere.[16] For the present purposes, it is not necessary to consider such theories.

In the following text with gray background, I derive a special version of Bell's Inequality using only counting. Although it requires some close reasoning, it is worth working your way through. However, if you do not enjoy such arguments, you can skip to the end of the text with gray background without missing any conclusions.

Using the notation above and Einstein's assumptions, we can develop an interpretation of the experiment. In case 1, the tests are identical on the left and right, both resonators pass or fail the tests together, and they score equally well on all three tests. From this perfect correlation, we can infer with certainty that, at least when the tests are the same for both, the resonators have the same characteristics. Since the bells are matched pairs of resonators, this correlation is hardly surprising. Quality control was bad in Tsongkhapa's time, but still the resonators were paired—at least when the tests were the same as in case 1 data.

We can infer more than this because the resonators never "know" until it is too late to be of any use whether they are both taking the same test or not. (We used locality to establish the complete isolation of one independent and random test selection on one side from that on the other.) Next, employ the critical Einstein separability assumption: "the mutually independent existence (the 'being-thus') of spatially distant things." Although separability is simple and reasonable, it is the pivotal assumption. Separability or mutually independent existence, with the isolation of the resonators and the perfect correlation for test combinations A–A, B–B, and C–C, implies that the resonators must always have identical attributes for the artistic style, bronze content, and construction strength, although we can only perform one test at a time on a resonator. We deduce this from case 1 data and the assumptions by noting that, if the pair did not always have identical attributes, it would occasionally happen that one resonator passes an artistic test while the other fails—something that never occurs.

Now, since the resonators always have identical attributes, if we make a different measurement in the left and right rooms, we are in effect simultaneously measuring two dissimilar properties of the resonators—something standard quantum mechanics claims is impossible. (Maybe the bell salesman really has a clever scheme that defeats complementarity and satisfies Tsongkhapa's need for more detailed analysis!)

I use the following shorthand notation for the relevant property set of the resonators: a+ b+ c+ means a resonator will pass all three tests (artistic, bronze, and construction), while a+ b- c+ means that the resonator will pass the artistic test, fail the bronze test, and pass the construction test. (Uppercase letters as in A–B or C–C are for test selections in the left and right rooms, while lowercase letters as in a+ b- c+ are for attributes of a given resonator.) Then there are eight possible property sets: a+ b+ c+, a+ b+ c-, a+ b- c+, a- b+ c+, a- b- c-, a- b- c+, a- b+ c-, and a+ b- c-. *Assuming locality and Einstein separability (mutually independent existence), analysis of case 1 data shows that both members of each pair of resonators always have the same property sets.* With these assumptions, they must be fully matched pairs. Now let's discuss case 2 data.

Case 2 Data

Here the tests in each room are *different*. Then the testing combinations are A–B, A–C, B–C, B–A, C–A, and C–B; and we experimentally find that *one-fourth* of the tests give the same results (both sides pass or fail).

With this data, our task is now to deduce what results should follow from our assumptions for case 2. I first analyze the *possible* outcomes of the experiment and thereby provide a framework for evaluating the data. Correlation Table 4.2 shows seven columns. The first column on the left lists the possible property sets, while the next six columns give the correlation results for the six possible test combinations for case 2. Each entry in the table is either an "S" or a "D," indicating that the property set for that test combination gives either the same (both pass or fail) or different test results.

Properties	A-B	A-C	B-C	B-A	C-A	C-B
	Test Combinations					
a+b+c+	S	S	S	S	S	S
a+b+c-	S	**<u>D</u>**	D	S	D	D
a+b-c+	D	S	D	D	S	D
a-b+c+	D	D	S	D	D	S
a-b-c-	S	S	S	S	S	S
a-b-c+	S	D	D	S	D	D
a-b+c-	D	S	D	D	S	D
a+b-c-	D	D	S	D	D	S

CORRELATION TABLE 4.2

For example, the bold, underlined entry in the table indicates that, when the property set for the resonators is a+ b+ c- and the test combination is A–C, then the test results are different (the resonator on the left passes, while the one on the right fails). I encourage you to check a few entries to be sure they are correct.

We can make an already easy counting task even easier if we realize there is much redundancy in the table. The redundancy results from our being interested only in whether the test results were the same or different on each side. Therefore, we do not discriminate between getting + + or - - , they both yield S, nor between + - or - +, which both yield D. This makes the entire table three duplicates of any one quarter of the table. For example, the upper left quadrant is identical to the lower right quadrant and so on.

Having laid out Table 4.2, we can do some simple counting. I take two cases to bracket the extreme possibilities of interest.

Since the test selections are independent and random, for a given property set, the six test combinations must occur equally often. After all, this is what a random selection of test combinations means.

First, assume a *uniform population* of bells—each property set is equally likely. In other words, in a uniform population, it is just as likely that a bell will have a property set a+ b- c- as a+ b+ c+ or any other property set. With this uniform population, each entry in the table has an equal statistical weight. As we can see from the table, the same number of Ds as Ss occurs in any one quarter of it. Thus, if we tested a large group of bells with this uniform population, they would give the same test results exactly one-half of the time.

Second, to complete the analysis, assume a nonuniform population with no resonators having either a+ b+ c+ or a- b- c- property sets, but the other sets are equally represented. This eliminates those property sets that always give Ss for all test combinations. For every remaining property set, in a given quarter of the table, there is one S and two Ds. Thus, resonators with these property sets (our nonuniform population) will always score the same results only one-third of the time. If you think about it for a moment, you'll see that this nonuniform population gives the minimum number of sames or "Ss."

Since any other population must lie between these extremes, any combination of property sets will give the same results at least one-third of the time when the tests are different. In other words, with different tests, it is impossible to get less than a one-third correlation.

Assuming only locality, mutually independent existence, and case 1 data, then any possible population of bells must yield the same test results at least one-third *of the time when the tests given on each side are different (case 2). This is a special version of Bell's Inequality.*

With this theoretical analysis in hand, let's return to the monastery. There case 2 measurements (when the test combinations are different) show that resonators score the same results exactly *one-fourth* of the time.

Since Tsongkhapa and his assistants carefully give the tests to so many resonators, they have excellent statistics. There is no doubt that the test results they measure are the same exactly *one-fourth* of the time when the tests on each side are different. Wait! This is impossible! According to the counting exercise we just did, any possible population of bells must give a minimum correlation of *one-third* when the test combinations are different. This experimental violation of Bell's Inequality implies that one or both of the critical assumptions of locality and mutually independent existence (Einstein separability) must be wrong. It also shows that the bell salesman could not beat complementarity after all because he could not reliably measure two properties at once with this scheme.

If we replace the resonator pairs with correlated photon pairs and the pass-fail tests with randomly selected polarization measurements perpendicular to the line of flight of the photons, then we have the actual experiments violating Bell's Inequality and confirming the predictions of standard quantum mechanics.[17] The correlations are not dependent upon distance. They grow neither stronger nor weaker with the separation between the left and right measurements.

Physicists find this analysis compelling for several reasons. First, the assumptions of locality and mutually independent existence or Einstein separability are extremely reasonable assumptions. Einstein goes so far as to say that "[w]ithout such an assumption of the mutually independent existence (the 'being-thus') of spatially distant things, an assumption which originates in everyday thought, physical thought in the sense familiar to us would not be possible." Second, the logic and mathematics of the analysis are well understood and beyond reproach. Third, physicists have repeated the original elegant and difficult experiments in a variety of forms with the same results. As I mentioned above, the experiments are even performed by undergraduates at Colgate University. In short, from very fundamental principles with a minimum of reasoning, Bell's Inequality has been carefully derived and then repeatedly shown to be violated by very convincing experiments.

Since there are so many steps leading to the experimental violation of Bell's Inequality, let me provide the briefest summary of how we got here. The story begins in 1935 with Einstein in the EPR paper, which asserted that quantum mechanics was incomplete because it did not allow for the full specification of complementary properties even though they were "elements of reality." Bohr quickly responded by saying that you could not posit definite properties of objects independent of the entire measurement situation. Einstein and others were not convinced, and the debates continued. A landmark occurred in 1964 when John Bell used the locality principle and Einstein separability (inherent existence in Middle Way language) to develop a statistical inequality for correlated particle pairs. (I derived a simple version of Bell's Inequality above.) In the next two decades, progressively more convincing experimental refutations of the Bell inequality were performed, while the predictions of quantum mechanics were precisely confirmed. The last decade or so has seen nonlocality employed for the building of sophisticated cryptographic schemes. Nonlocality is also at the heart of quantum computing, the next big leap in computing power.

What Went Wrong?

Given that both the experimental protocol and the theoretical analysis are sound, what assumptions are wrong? The prevailing view believes in locality since it pervades all physics, but relaxes the demand for Einstein separability or "mutually·independent existence," especially since quantum mechanics avoids this assumption and yet accurately predicts the proper correlations. So my hero Einstein is simply wrong when he says, "But on one supposition we should, in my opinion, absolutely hold fast: the real factual situation of the system S2 is independent of what is done with the system S1, which is spatially separated from the former."[18] We may not assume that objects such as correlated photons (or bell resonators) have well-defined natures independent of experiments performed far away (even light years away!). Because of the locality principle, it is also wrong to believe in faster-than-light communication between the left and right sides.

If we were, on the other hand, to relax the assumption of locality and allow instantaneous action at distance, then we still could not say "the real factual situation of the system S2 is independent of what is done with the system S1, which is spatially separated from the former." With instantaneous action at a distance, the "real factual situation" becomes meaningless since something infinitely far away can instantaneously affect it—hardly what we would call having an independent existence. In standard quantum mechanics, there is no instantaneous action at a distance because there are no independently existing objects that communicate superluminally, that is, faster than the speed of light. Nevertheless, the system of correlated photons of arbitrary separation acts more like one system than any classical system.

Communication from one end of a classical system to another can only happen at the speed of light or less. This type of communication could not give the measured correlations for our experiment. We are seeing here a mysterious level of interconnectedness that is more interdependent, more profoundly related, than we can imagine.

In summary, nonlocality is asking us to revise completely our ideas about objects, to remove a pervasive projection we have upon nature. We can no longer consider objects as independently existing entities, localized in well-defined regions of space-time. Nonlocality teaches us that the properties at one location instantaneously depend upon properties found at arbitrarily large distances. As stated after figure 4.2, with its objects made of dotted lines and connections of solid lines, talking quantum particles would say, "I exist in a well-defined way because of my relationship to other particles. I have no independent existence." Although Middle Way emptiness is a more inclusive principle than quantum nonlocality, the Middle Way denial of independent or inherent existence precisely parallels the arguments in physics that establish quantum nonlocality.

The correlated particles are interconnected in ways not even conceivable using ideas from classical physics, which is largely a refinement and extrapolation from our normal macroscopic sense-functioning. It is worth repeating that the interconnections spoken about here are not like those in classical physics, those limited by the speed of light. These are instantaneous interconnections. These quantum correlations reveal that nature is *noncausally* unified in ways we only dimly understand. We are so used to conceiving of a world of isolated and independently existing objects that it is very difficult for us to understand what the experiments are telling us about nature. They are truly confronting us with the demand for a major paradigm shift at the foundations of science and philosophy—one with enormous implications for fields well beyond the boundaries of science and philosophy. Despite technological applications of nonlocality for such things as cryptography and quantum computing, it will take time for the view of nature implied by nonlocality to be understood fully and to penetrate the collective psyche.

Before turning to some implications of nonlocality for peace, a few points should be stressed. First, not all quantum systems show this deep kind of interconnectedness. Nevertheless, nonlocality is pervasive in quantum mechanics.

Second, quantum mechanics teaches us that we must avoid viewing entities as isolated with intrinsic properties independent of the observational conditions. As Bohr says, "I advocate the application of the word *phenomenon* exclusively to refer to the observations obtained under specified circumstances, including an account of the whole experimental arrangement."[19] In Middle Way language, Bohr is telling us that quantum objects cannot be understood in isolation, independent of the "whole experimental arrangement." In other words, they lack independent existence and are in fact dependently related to the details of our measurement apparatus, even if we never actually carry out the measurements.

Third, although I do not discuss it here, these faster-than-light interconnections cannot be used to send information at faster than the speed of light. This follows from the essentially statistical nature of quantum mechanics. Therefore, you cannot get rich selling this idea to the U.S. Defense Department!

Fourth, even if you follow each step of the argument, there is an unsettling quality to it. In essence, the argument simply shows that Einstein separability or mutually independent existence does not hold. However, it does not more fully characterize the quality or nature of the interconnectedness. In other words, this is a negative argument with precise parallels to typical Middle Way debates. Einstein first carefully defined the "object of negation," here, Einstein separability, mutually independent existence, or inherent existence. Then, through careful reasoning, we derived above a special form of Bell's Inequality. Finally, by appeal to rigorously controlled experiments, the inequality was seen not to hold, thereby destroying Einstein separability or what the Middle Way calls inherent or independent existence. However, it is important to notice that the argument and experiments do not replace our old view of objects with "being-thus" or mutually independent existence with some positive view. Just as in the case of traditional Middle Way arguments for emptiness, there is a massive negation without substituting some new positive principle, a deeper reality beyond nonlocality. What most of us are unconsciously searching for is some mechanistic explanation for the correlations. However, this is merely a reversion to an incorrect view of a set of steps made up of inherently existent entitles of some kind.

It is an unprecedented event in physics when a philosophic principle of such fundamental importance as independent or inherent existence is carefully defined, quantitatively analyzed, and experimentally shown not to exist. It truly is a form of experimental metaphysics. Here we can clearly see that the mind projected independent existence into the particles, but the experimental violation of Bell's Inequalities shows that nature refuses to accept the projection. It is also important to notice that the Bell analysis depends only upon the assumptions of locality and Einstein separablity (mutually independent existence) and is independent of the structure of quantum mechanics. Thus, any future replacement for today's version of quantum mechanics will have to incorporate nonlocality in the new version. In other words, this analysis shows that nonlocality is a genuine feature of nature independent of our present theory of quantum mechanics. It is even more extraordinary that such experimental metaphysics so closely connects with the philosophic heart of Tibetan Buddhism.

Nevertheless, pairs of correlated quantum particles are a long way from the realities of daily life where the principle of emptiness applies. Therefore, in the next section, I move from an intellectual discussion of emptiness, so powerfully displayed in quantum mechanics, to a practical expression of it in compassion and daily life.

Emptiness and Compassion

In the introduction to this chapter, I quoted the physicist David Bohm who suggested that one of the key factors giving rise to the pervasive strife between peoples and nations is "a kind of thought that treats things as inherently divided, disconnected . . . [where] each part is considered to be essentially independent and self-existent." Because quantum nonlocality teaches us just the opposite of this view, it is truly the physics of peace. Let me attempt to deepen this idea by returning to the Middle Way.

The Middle Way rests on the two great pillars of emptiness and compassion. A realization of emptiness, of our profound interdependence with each other and the world surrounding us, decreases egotism and increases the genuine concern for all life. If I truly lack independent existence, if my deepest reality is one of mutual dependence upon other lifeforms and my surroundings, then how can I be concerned with just me? How can I focus on the needs of merely one intersection of the innumerable dependency relations defining all persons and things? If each person is an interdependent cell in the body of humanity, how then can I focus on the desires of just one and thereby harm the whole? Of course, we have no rational justification for our self-centeredness and self-cherishing. Nevertheless, those firmly ingrained tendencies are painfully difficult to uproot.

The principle of emptiness, whether it comes from traditional Middle Way arguments or appreciating quantum nonlocality, has a deep resonance with the ancient South African principle of *Ubuntu*, "I am because you are." My very existence requires your existence. There is no such thing as isolated or independent existence, whether we speak of particles or people. Rather than self-existing individuals we are expressions of our mutual connectedness to each other, the community, and the larger environment. It follows then that, if you suffer, I suffer. If you are happy, then I am happy.

Archbishop Desmond Tutu has revised the principle of *Ubuntu* as a means of bringing about reconciliation and healing in a country long divided by vicious apartheid and deep hatred. He states, "A self-sufficient human being is subhuman. I have gifts that you do not have, so consequently, I am unique—you have gifts that I do not have, so you are unique. God has made us so that we will need each other. We are made for a delicate network of interdependence."[20] Although references to God often make Buddhists uncomfortable, the reference to our "delicate network of interdependence" certainly echoes the principle of emptiness, while still affirming our uniqueness on the conventional level.

The greatest obstacle to fully appreciating the wisdom of *Ubuntu* or of emptiness is our inveterate and unconscious belief in the independent or inherent existence of our own egos. Practicing compassion weakens this false belief blocking the doorway to the wisdom of emptiness. Thus, if we can truly practice compassion, if we can show a deep and genuine concern for both our fellow humans and the environment in which we live, then our understanding of emptiness, of our far-reaching interconnectedness must grow. In this way, the two pillars of the Middle Way have a synergistic relationship in encouraging us to take more responsibility for the welfare of all sentient beings, the true foundation for all peace work, whether personal or global. I quoted the Dalai Lama in the previous chapter as saying, "Foolish selfish people are always thinking of themselves, and the result is negative. Wise selfish people think of others, help others as much as they can, and the result is that they too receive benefit."

In part because of the Dalai Lama's focus on compassion, I have always wanted to understand more deeply the connection between compassion and emptiness. I actually want to derive compassion from emptiness, to see how it logically flows like a result in physics from an understanding of the lack of inherent existence. Perhaps my years of doing theoretical physics predispose me to this approach. Emptiness certainly implies the need for compassion and, as I discussed toward the end of the previous chapter, understanding how we and others are caught in the process of projecting inherent existence leads us to universal compassion. In this way, knowledge leads to compassion or love. Nevertheless, it never quite worked on an emotional level for me to derive compassion from intellectual analysis alone. Perhaps my desire for a derivation of compassion from emptiness also assumes that emptiness is the superior principle from which the lesser (compassion) is derived. That is clearly not the correct view of these two pillars of the Middle Way.

Fortunately, life has shown me a little about how to approach emptiness through the heart, how to take in the pain of the other person and thereby make a deep feeling connection to them. I then become more open to them and the reality of their suffering. In this way, rather than approach compassion through the physics of peace, I try to assimilate our profound interconnections by opening to the suffering of others. The goal is to expand this openness to include everybody with a similar affliction and, still further, to include all suffering beings. Such openness to suffering softens my habitual focus on my ego and its needs. The connection is through the heart, not through the head. This kind of openness leads to a feeling realization of emptiness, to appreciating how connections to others establish my identity, to understanding how, without these relationships, there is no "I" at all, how "I am because you are." Here is an expression of compassion leading to a deeper understanding of emptiness or interconnectedness, of love leading to knowledge. I will try to show how this can occur through a little personal experience from a couple of years ago.

The Thief as Guru

I am traveling for several weeks in Europe giving lectures and workshops. Despite the terrific extroversion of such activities, I am enjoying the periods of isolation and introversion that travel provides. I have finished reading the books I brought from home, so in a London airport I purchase *Ethics for the New Millennium* by the Dalai Lama. Although I have heard all of these ideas before, both through reading and oral instruction from a variety of Tibetan teachers, the book's direct, clear, and simple message inspires me. With a minimum of technical language, the Dalai Lama shows how our happiness and genuine ethics follow from our effort to alleviate suffering. The root of all ethical action must be our sincere effort to reduce suffering. These well-known ideas have been electrifying me for the last couple of days.

After about an hour of reading in the Barcelona airport, I stretch my legs with a walk among the fancy shops. I continue to reflect on these ideas as I return to the departure gate. On my way toward the departing line, I sincerely vow to work more intensely on practicing compassion. I tell myself, "I can surely do much better."

Suddenly, out of the corner of my eye, I see a fearsome fistfight about twenty meters from my departure line. A policeman and another man are furiously pummeling each other. The policeman is on the floor and getting the worst of it. I instantly decide that this is harming the other man even more than the policeman, so I sprint to the fight. I grab the man by the shoulders and pull hard, but I cannot separate them. In desperation, I come up behind the man, wrap my right arm over his right shoulder and pull him against my chest, grasp his left arm, and give a mighty heave. As the two men separate, the man pinned against my chest gives a powerful two-legged thrust to the policeman's chest knocking off his badge and throwing him flat on his back. The man and I land in a heap with me on my back and him on top of me.

I hug him tightly to my chest, while we struggle awkwardly to a sitting position. He is breathing like a racehorse. His heart is pounding. I feel his beard stubble against my left jaw. Astonishingly, the policeman jumps up and runs to the far end of the terminal and telephones for help. I am very unhappy being left clutching the fighter, but soon other people come to restrain him. I say to him with surprising tenderness, "Just let it go. It is not worth it." These seem like strangely ineffective words, especially since he is unlikely to understand English. I notice that he is about thirty years old, the same age as my oldest son.

In a few minutes, more police arrive and handcuff the man. I get up from the floor and return to the departure line. My tailbone is sore from landing on it. Somebody hands me the Dalai Lama book that had fallen on the floor early in the struggle. As I walk back to the line I think, "The cop didn't even say '*Gracias*.'"

Standing in line, a deep sadness overwhelms me. I have to fight the desire to sob uncontrollably. Embarrassed to cry in the departure line, I ask myself, "What is this powerful sadness?" Somebody ahead of me in the line tells me that the policeman caught the man picking somebody's pocket.

That overwhelming sadness has long mystified me. At first, I thought my sadness was due to the policeman not recognizing or appreciating my effort. "I risked physical harm to minimize the pounding that policeman was taking. I want at least a 'Thank you.'" Even more, it embarrasses me to confess my desire to be lionized as a hero. Realizing that my motivation was not entirely pure grieves me, especially when, in the book that was just inspiring me, the Dalai Lama writes, "When we give with the underlying motive of inflating the image others have of us—to gain renown and have them think of us as virtuous or holy—we defile the act. In that case, what we are practicing is not generosity but self-aggrandizement."[21]

My motivation was not entirely pure, but there surely is more to it. When I clutched that man in my arms, besides feeling his heart beating wildly, his gasping breath, and even the scratch of his whiskers, I also felt his suffering. A genuine tenderness welled up in me towards him. More than physical intimacy, I directly contacted the broken life that led to the event, a brokenness that was likely to continue well after the prison term that was sure to follow. It is one thing to reflect quietly on suffering while reading a book and another to feel it squirming against your body. I did not have to think about nonlocality in quantum mechanics to make a connection with this man. I only had to be open to his suffering. The Dalai Lama writes:

> When we enhance our sensitivity toward others' suffering through deliberately opening ourselves up to it, it is believed that we can gradually extend our compassion to the point where the individual feels so moved by even the subtlest suffering of others that they come to have an overwhelming sense of responsibility toward those others. This causes the one who is compassionate to dedicate themselves entirely to helping others overcome both their suffering and the causes of their

> suffering. In Tibetan, this ultimate level of attainment is called *nying je chenmo*, literally "great compassion."[22]

I am certainly far from the advanced level of *nying je chenmo*, but I have seen how opening, even unwittingly, toward the suffering of others makes me appreciate the profound interconnectedness we all share. Such appreciation through the heart complements the intellectual apprehension of quantum nonlocality and emptiness. That man, accused of being a pickpocket, could have been my son. As much as Einstein and Bohr educated my intellectual understanding, he educated my heart and moved me a little closer to a union of love and knowledge.

5. A Quantum Mechanical Challenge to Tibetan Buddhism

From Agreement to Challenge

In the previous chapter, we saw the extraordinarily close connections between quantum nonlocality and Middle Way emptiness. We had a chance to see how the mind projects independent existence into matter and how nature refuses the projection, as revealed by numerous and varied experiments. Just as in the Middle Way, nothing replaces the independent existence we had falsely believed necessary. (Recall that emptiness is a nonaffirming negation.) No mechanical model for nonlocality exists. This would necessarily involve positing independent entities, which we have just worked so hard to banish. We are just left with the truth of the deep interdependency and interconnectedness of the pairs of correlated quantum particles. While quantum mechanics does not directly address the nature of persons, the Middle Way certainly does—by denying them independent existence, along with the rest of the universe.

As I have sketched, our profound interconnectedness to each other and our environment, which is another way of speaking about emptiness, implies the necessity for universal compassion. In Buddhism, philosophic principles always have moral consequences.

While emptiness and quantum nonlocality seem to embrace like two close friends, this chapter will show that, with respect to causality, physics and Buddhism seem like friends having a serious disagreement. I believe that real friendship can sustain disagreement, can accommodate opposing views and still hold together. If we can be friends only when we agree and our alliance easily falls apart when we disagree, then our friendship is shallow. Part of deep friendship is a commitment to work through disagreements, differences of viewpoints, and even sustain the friendship when each partner holds contrary views.

I believe that the deep friendship between quantum mechanics and the Middle Way discussed so far can sustain the disagreements in this chapter, even though they are fundamental. My hope is that the disagreement will cause each partner in the friendship to think more deeply, to understand the opposing views more fully, and that this understanding will provide the ground from which a reconciling view could grow.

While appreciating the many deep connections between Buddhism and science is clearly important, it may even be more important for our understanding of both Buddhism and science to see precisely where they are in conflict. For it is often the case that in conflict we understand the opposing positions more clearly, whether these positions be between individuals, nations, or worldviews. This chapter, therefore, explores the conflict between Buddhism and physics at a deep level. Now, let us see how causality is at the center of the disagreement.

Causality

Causality is at the heart of all varieties of Buddhism. Our past actions are the causes of our present condition. Whatever excellences or failings we have now are the effects of our previous actions, in this life and previous lives. Because of the universality of the law of cause and effect, we can also take the right actions now and in the future become buddhas, perfectly enlightened beings of infinite wisdom and compassion. In short, our present condition is the result of past actions and, thanks to the law of cause and effect, we can positively influence the future. In Tibetan Buddhism, the universality of cause and effect is one of the principal arguments for establishing emptiness, the ultimate truth. As we saw in earlier chapters, emptiness also provides intellectual support for universal compassion. In this way, cause and effect are central to both the practice and the theory of Tibetan Buddhism.

The Dalai Lama's extended meeting with physicists at one of the Mind and Life Series conferences in 1997 resulted in the book *The New Physics and Cosmology: Dialogues with the Dalai Lama*.[1] The editor of that book, Arthur Zajonc, told me that the Dalai Lama was particularly uncomfortable with the idea of noncausality in quantum mechanics. Given the pivotal importance of causality in Buddhism, this is not surprising.

In a more recent book, *The Universe in a Single Atom: The Convergence of Science and Spirituality*, we can directly see the Dalai Lama's discomfort with any lack of causality. It is especially noticeable in his discussion of Darwinian evolution, which he largely supports.

To appreciate why the Dalai Lama is uncomfortable with some features of Darwinian evolution, we must first appreciate that evolution is a two-step process. First, there are random mutations of the DNA molecules. These random mutations, which are largely transcription errors in generating new DNA, are governed by quantum mechanics. They are, thus, truly random, with no well-defined causes for individual events. Second, these random mutations, which may generate DNA that is only infinitesimally different from its predecessors, then compete for survival in the environment. Most new forms have less reproductive success than their predecessors do, but some have a competitive advantage, and they succeed. Through these slow, infinitesimally small changes, filled with extraordinary inefficiency and suffering, the evolution of species occurs. It is important to appreciate how Darwinian evolution is rooted in a deep form of randomness, which I explore more fully in this chapter. The Dalai Lama finds the first random step to be the most difficult to accept. He writes, "From the Buddhist perspective, the idea of these mutations being purely random events is deeply unsatisfying for a theory that purports to explain the origin of life."[2]

In private communication, Alan Wallace, one of the scholar/translators at the Mind and Life Series with the most extensive discussion of Darwinian evolution, told me that the Dalai Lama is most concerned that science only accepts physical causality.[3] Of course, physical causality, which must involve measurable laboratory effects, is the only kind that science would admit. Nevertheless, all Buddhists schools hold that nonphysical influences, such as *karma*, are essential for understanding many processes, especially human evolution. Since nonphysical influences cannot be measured in the laboratory, here is a fundamental divergence. (Remember Richard Feynman's definition from the first chapter: "The principle of science, the definition, almost, is the following: The test of all knowledge is experiment. Experiment is the sole judge of scientific 'truth.'"[4]) Given the present formulation of both science and Buddhism, we cannot solve this fundamental divergence now. Nevertheless, we can take the first step toward resolution by clarifying the divergence. I do that by discussing causality in Buddhism, giving an example of nonphysical influences in the Middle Way, discussing physical noncausality in quantum mechanics, and then returning to the question of Darwinian evolution.

This discomfort with a lack of causality in quantum mechanics is widely shared in Tibetan Buddhism. For example, within the last two years, I had a very lively hour-long discussion with three *geshes* at the Namgyal monastery in Ithaca, New York, on the subject of causality in quantum mechanics. Largely because of language difficulties, our discussion did not get far, but it was clear that we were dealing with foundational issues in both physics and Buddhism.

Because of the Dalai Lama's interest in the topic and that exciting exchange with the *geshes*, we organizers of a Buddhism and Science Dialogue at the Namgyal monastery decided upon the theme of "Comparative Views of Causation" for a conference at Cornell University in October of 2005. This chapter is a significantly expanded version of my presentation at that conference.

Our goal at the conference, and mine here too, was to reach out across disciplinary boundaries and be as comprehensible as possible to nonexperts, while still carefully treating the fundamental issues. Here I start with a discussion of causality in the Middle Way embedded within the context of Newtonian physics. Although causality plays an especially prominent role in all forms of Buddhism, to achieve the most tightly focused comparison with causality in quantum mechanics, I restrict myself to the view of the Middle Way Consequence School of Tibetan Buddhism, which I have been consistently abbreviating in this book as Middle Way. I then move on to the more mysterious lack of causality in quantum mechanics and briefly sketch some of its implications. As in the previous chapter, I place some slightly more technical material that is not essential to the argument within a gray background. You can start reading it. If you enjoy it, then continue; otherwise, you can skip it and still get the main points.

Middle Way and Newtonian Causality

The Middle Way analyzes causality into substantial causes and cooperative conditions. Let us go into the undergraduate physics lab to see how this works. Figure 5.1 diagrams one of the simplest laboratory exercises in our introductory course at Colgate University. This lab has a spring gun sitting on a table of height H. A student puts a ball bearing into the spring gun, pulls back the spring, and shoots the ball. The ball flies through the air as shown by the dashed line and hits a large piece of carbon paper taped to the floor. The bearing's mark on this paper allows a careful measurement of the distance, D, that the ball travels before hitting the floor. We need not discuss the physics in this lab, except to say that it affords a test of several laws of Newtonian physics and allows for a measurement of the acceleration due to gravity, $g = 9.8 \text{ m/sec}^2$.

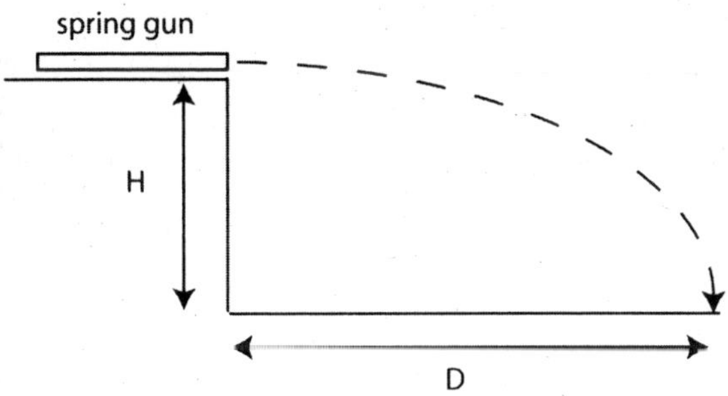

FIGURE 5.1. *Elementary lab setup*

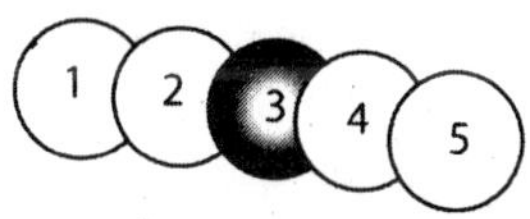

FIGURE 5.2. *Ball in flight*

Imagine that we use a high-speed camera to take several pictures of the ball in flight. The five individual images shown in figure 5.2 are taken only a tiny fraction of a second apart. Let us consider picture 3, the ball bearing at time t_3, which I have shaded so that it can serve as a reference point for our discussion. Notice picture 2 at t_2, a little time before t_3, and picture 4 at t_4, a little time after t_3. Let's say that picture 3 is the ball bearing in the present moment at time t_3. What the Middle Way calls the substantial cause of the ball at time t_3 is the ball at time t_2 because the ball at t_3 is a continuation of the substantial nature of the ball at t_2. Substantiality here means having a well-defined nature or type. Thus, ball 2 is the substantial cause, and ball 3 is the substantial effect. For them, the ball bearing is constantly changing from moment to moment—not just because it is moving through the air but also because its empty nature implies that each particle of which it is composed is constantly coming into existence and then going out of existence in the very next moment. In each moment, all objects and subjects are undergoing production, abiding, and disintegrating. (In the Middle Way, according to Geshe Thupten Kunkhen, a moment lasts for 1/360 of the time it takes to snap a finger.[5] Such a time of approximately 10^{-4} seconds is very long by atomic standards, where typical time scales are more like 10^{-8} seconds, or even longer in comparison to nuclear time scales of 10^{-22} seconds.)

For the Middle Way, the deep interdependencies and interconnections constituting an object guarantee its impermanence in both a gross and subtle sense. Figure 5.2 tries to show this with pictures of the ball taken at slightly different times. This idea of a ball bearing continuously transforming itself is consistent with our present scientific understanding of the dynamic state of the matter of the ball. Although it may appear to be the same ball from moment to moment, we know that the underlying matter is continuously transforming itself. It is only the coarseness of our sense functioning that gives rise to our false belief in the constancy of the ball bearing.

Just as the ball bearing at t_2 is the substantial cause of the ball bearing at t_3, we can say that ball 4 is the substantial continuation of ball 3. It may help to consider an example that is closer to home. The substantial cause of your consciousness now is the state of your consciousness in the immediately previous moment, just as your consciousness now will be the substantial cause of your consciousness in the next moment. For the Middle Way, all functioning things (something that produces an effect), from various types of consciousnesses to elementary particles or galaxies, have substantial causes. With these terms, we can more formally define a substantial cause as a main producer of a substantial effect (a functioning thing), which is a continuum of a similar type.[6] The emphasis here is on the production of an effect that is of a similar nature (or a continuum of a similar type) to the producer or cause.

Returning to the ball bearing, we can also say that the steel from which it is made is also a substantial cause.

Now consider the *cooperative conditions* or, as some call them, the *circumstantial causes.* We can say that the milling or grinding process in the manufacturing of the ball bearings is the cooperative condition or the circumstantial cause of the ball bearing. Clearly, the ball bearing is not substantially continuous with the milling and polishing it undergoes but with the underlying steel or the immediately prior instance of the ball.

Nevertheless, without the cooperative conditions of the milling process, there would be no ball bearing. Some would consider that the laws of physics determine the ball's trajectory and thus are cooperating conditions or circumstantial causes of its evolution in space and time. I certainly agree that these nonmaterial laws of physics are not substantially continuous with the ball. However, I consider the equations of motion as models or descriptions of the ball's dynamics, not as causes that compel, influence, or determine a ball's trajectory.

Now we are ready to add the idea of *direct* and *indirect* to substantial causes and cooperative conditions. In figure 5.2, ball 2 at t_2 is the *direct substantial cause* of ball 3 at t_3. However, ball 1 at t_1 is the *indirect substantial cause* of ball 3. In the same way, ball 2 is the indirect substantial cause of ball 4 at t_4. You can also consider ball 3 to be the indirect substantial effect of ball 1 or ball 4 to be the indirect substantial effect of ball 2. So indirect just means at least one step removed from the present effect.

We could also say that the order to the factory for the ball bearings is the indirect cooperative condition for the balls. Somebody makes a formal order to the factory for ball bearings, the raw materials (substantial causes) are gathered together, and then the ball bearings are milled. We thus have the sequence: factory order for ball bearings (indirect cooperative conditions), gathering together of the raw materials (gathering is an indirect cooperative condition, while the raw material is the indirect substantial cause), milling of the ball bearings (a later, but still indirect cooperative condition), the ball bearing at its birth (the indirect substantial cause of the ball bearing in our lab), etc.

You can easily see that we have an enormous number of direct and indirect substantial causes and cooperating conditions. In fact, we could say that the conceiving of the laboratory exercise is an indirect cooperative condition for the order to the factory, while the PhD of the physics professor is the indirect cooperative cause of his being a professor, which gives him the responsibility for designing the laboratory exercise, and on and on we go. We thus have an indefinitely large interconnected web of indirect and direct substantial causes and cooperating conditions. Because of this intricate web of causes and conditions, the ball bearing, despite our naïve views about it, is completely void of independent or inherent existence. In other words, its myriad dependencies guarantee its emptiness and impermanence.

It is essential to appreciate that the Middle Way interpretation of causality stresses that all causes and effects are totally empty of inherent existence. Let me briefly consider how violating this condition would lead to a hopelessly incoherent notion of causality. Begin by considering any of the substantial causes/effects depicted in figure 5.2 to exist inherently or independently. Let us start with ball 3, the ball in the present moment. If that ball inherently exists, then its nature would be complete and self-contained entirely on its own. Its essence or deepest nature would need nothing outside itself to exist and be what it inherently is. It would exist from its own side, independent of conceptual designation. Then, by this very nature, it could not affect other entities (such as ball 4) or be affected by outside agents (such as ball 2). It would, thus, be neither a cause nor an effect but an entity frozen in its isolation, immutability, and impotence. The same reasoning applies to cooperative conditions, which are effective only through their very emptiness of inherent existence.

An important aspect of the Middle Way approach to causality is their unique understanding of disintegratedness as a functioning thing, a state of having disintegrated.[7] The Middle Way grounds its understanding in careful analysis of scripture and precise reasoning. Although disintegratedness plays a role in all phenomena, which by their very nature are impermanent, it is especially central to explaining how the effects of actions of one lifetime carry over to another. Here we are moving into the realm of nonphysical causation, something outside the domain of science. Let me give an example.

I am trying to concentrate on writing about disintegratedness and an annoying fly is buzzing around me and sometimes crawling on me. In a flash of anger, I whip my right hand from the keyboard and swat the fly on my left arm. In each moment, there is simultaneously production, abiding, and disintegration of impermanent phenomena—whether actions, objects, or states of consciousness. The causes for my fly swatting quickly disintegrate, as does the swatting. The question for the Middle Way is, if there is no inherently existing person, no independently existing core of Vic Mansfield continuing into the future and on into the next life, how then does the fly-killing *karma* continue into the future, including into a future lifetime? In other words, given that I do not inherently exist and am merely a constantly changing mental designation upon the impermanent mind and body, how do my actions, whether meritorious or evil, propagate into the future?

The Middle Way says that, in the immediate moment after the swatting, the action is in a state of disintegratedness, of having disintegrated. Here is the sequence. In the final stage of fly swatting there is production, abiding, and disintegration—followed in the next moment by disintegratedness of that event. In the next moment, that original disintegratedness disintegrates, giving rise to another disintegratedness. That disintegratedness, in turn, disintegrates and gives rise to a new disintegratedness. Each disintegratedness is the substantial cause of the following moment of disintegratedness. Each of the states of disintegratedness takes part in the moment-to-moment process of production, abiding, and disintegration. This process, which keeps producing new states of disintegratedness linked to the original action, continues until the appropriate substantial causes and cooperating conditions bring about the fruition of my fly-killing *karma*. Disintegratedness is a cause, an effect, and, therefore, a functioning thing, which links the original fly swatting to the later fruition of *karma*. This subtle idea at the heart of the Middle Way is, according to Geshe Thupten Kunkhen, a major topic for advanced debating in the Gelukba tradition.[8] Let me summarize this brief discussion by a diagram.

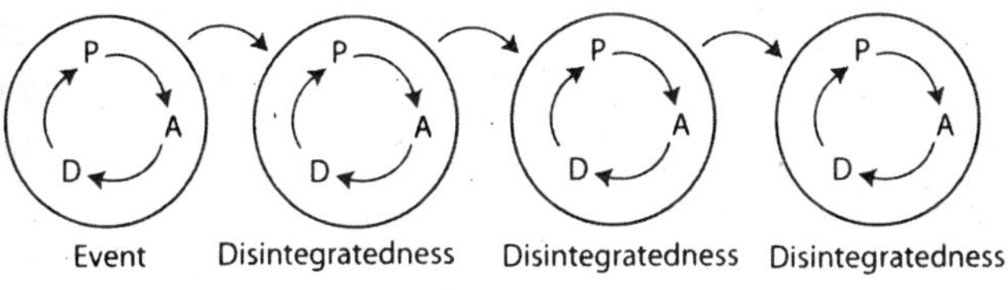

FIGURE 5.3. *Disintegratedness*

In figure 5.3, each circle is a moment. The first circle on the left represents the last moment of an event, say, my fly swatting. The letters P, A, and D inside each moment represent the simultaneous occurrence of production, abiding, and disintegration. The second circle represents the disintegratedness of the event, followed by another disintegratedness, another, and so forth. Each moment is the substantial cause of the moment following it. This process of ongoing disintegratedness accounts for the continuity of *karma*, without positing any inherently existent medium or entity for its propagation. In the case of the *karma* from fly swatting, since it must be able to carry over from one life to the next, this is a nonphysical process. Here is an example of nonphysical influences, which the Dalai Lama believes are essential for understanding human evolution. Yet, in that they are nonphysical, they are not subject to laboratory measurements and thus not susceptible to scientific analysis. Science and Buddhism must inevitably diverge at this point because of the nature of their deepest commitments.

However, this same process of disintegratedness carrying forward also applies to material transformations. For example, the extinguishing of the light of an oil lamp because of the exhaustion of the oil and wick is a traditional example of this process. This, of course, would be a physical expression of the functioning of disintegratedness.

From the lamp example, you can see that any phenomenon, which by its very nature must be continuously undergoing transformation, participates in the process of ongoing disintegratedness. What I find so lovely about this approach is how it accounts for continuity without any underlying inherent identity. As we will see below, a fundamental demand of quantum mechanics is to understand the continuity of evolution of a quantum system without positing any inherently existing material entity.

In chapter 3, I noted that there were three approaches to establishing emptiness: dependency upon causes and conditions, whole and part, and imputation by thought. The preceding pages just give more detail about how substantial causes and cooperative conditions imply emptiness, the complete lack of independent existence. Within this thoroughgoing emptiness, the principle of disintegratedness can then account for the continuity of both physical and nonphysical *karma*.

The intricate net of causes and cooperating conditions for every object expresses itself not only in the doctrine of emptiness but also in Tibetan Buddhist prayers before meals. Rather than just giving thanks for the food that sustains us and allows us to pursue spiritual practices, we can contemplate the causal network for each food item. For example, I give thanks for the oats that made up my breakfast cereal, for the soil and water on which the oats were grown, for all those that grew the oats, those that transported them, those that drilled the gas and oil in Saudi Arabia that became the fertilizer for the oats and the fuel that transported them, for the tractor that plowed the field for the oats, etc. Of course, there is no limit to this since we should consider the bowl itself. Then I give thanks for the bowl for my cereal, for the store clerk who sold me the bowl, for the spoon, and so forth until my cereal gets cold as I continue giving thanks for the indefinitely large web of causes for my breakfast.

THE WAVE–PARTICLE NATURE OF LIGHT

To prepare for a discussion of causality in quantum mechanics, we need to develop some elementary quantum ideas about the nature of light. Throughout this book, I appeal only to standard quantum theory as taught and verified in universities and industries worldwide; I avoid the numerous variations or nonstandard interpretations. Although standard theory and its Copenhagen interpretation have been frequently challenged, there are no generally agreed upon alternatives. It is important to appreciate that quantum mechanics is not only the foundation for much of the technology that we employ in daily life, such as this computer I'm writing with, but it is also the most exquisitely well-confirmed theory in the history of physics. There may be disagreements about the interpretation of the results of quantum mechanics, but there is no doubt about how to apply it and the breadth and accuracy of all its predictions. Any interpretations of quantum mechanics that I give here are the standard ones found in any of the modern textbooks that teach the subject.

A good place to start is with Colgate University's junior/senior-level quantum mechanics course for physics majors that I often teach. Such a course is standard fare in physics curricula across the world. However, thanks to my colleagues at Colgate, especially Professor Enrique Galvez, (shown in figure 5.4), we have an unusual course because there is an elegant and powerful laboratory component associated with it.[9] Because of the heavy intellectual demands of such quantum courses and the difficulty of designing and building engaging laboratory exercises, this standard course rarely, if ever, has a laboratory component. However, thanks to recent technological developments along with the ingenuity and creativity of Kiko (as Enrique is affectionately known), we have an extraordinarily beautiful set of labs that actually make measurements on single photons.

Being able to work with single photons is a great asset since we can then directly study elementary quantum events and all the strangeness they embody. To put these single photon measurements in context, imagine going outside on a clear night and staring up at the starry sky. Pick out a dim star, one close to your naked eye's detection limit. If you look at that star for just one second, your cornea collects approximately 100,000 photons. Each of these photons comes at an unpredictable time within that interval of one second. However, because we normally view so many photons per second, the quantum mechanical attributes of single photons are averaged out. In other words, our eyes are simply too coarse to see quantum mechanical features of individual photons. However, since these labs can work with individual photons, they elegantly demonstrate some of the deepest issues in quantum mechanics. Let me illustrate some quantum features of light by a nontechnical discussion of one of these labs.

FIGURE 5.4. *Kiko Galvez (from the family album)*

One of the great mysteries about light and matter is that they display both wave and particle natures. We can illustrate this beautifully with some of our lab equipment. Let's start with what is called a beam splitter, shown in figure 5.5.

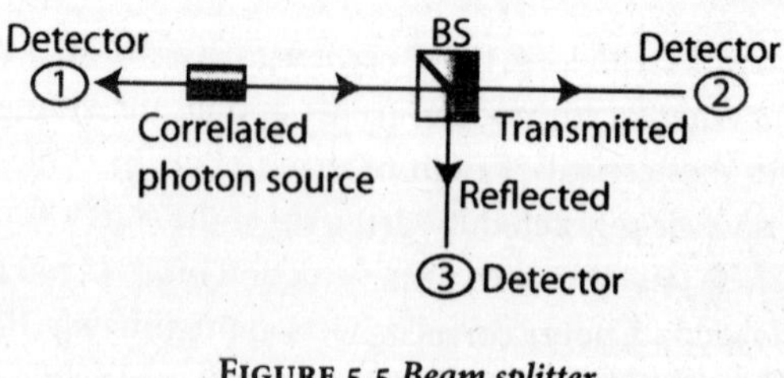

FIGURE 5.5 *Beam splitter*

Start on the left with the correlated source of photons, which emits identical, "entangled" photons in opposite directions, the kind of photon pairs we met in the experimental violation of Bell's Inequality in the previous chapter. An entangled pair of photons is like a set of identical twins or set of Tibetan bells, correlated in every way. However, a photon is a quantum of light, a fixed amount of energy, with complementary wave and particle natures, so it inherently has the complementarity I artificially imposed on the Tibetan bells. (Recall that the artistic merit of the bells was complementary to their bronze content and construction strength.) The photon directed to the left enters detector 1, while an identical photon directed to the right enters a beam splitter, abbreviated by BS.

The beam splitter transmits half of the input light and reflects the other half, somewhat like sunglasses with a reflective coating. Half of the input light is transmitted to detector 2 while the other half is reflected into detector 3. If light were strictly a wave phenomenon, we would find that, every time we get a signal in detector 2, we would also get one in detector 3. You can understand this by imagining a beach with a partially submerged breakwater. When water waves hit the breakwater, some of the wave energy would roll over the breakwater and some would be reflected. Returning to detectors 2 and 3, we find that, in a given time interval, each detector registers the same number of counts (identical sharp pulses corresponding to capturing individual photons). This implies that the beam splitter reflects and transmits equal amounts of energy. It seems to indicate that, although photons are generating sharp pulses, they are simultaneously exhibiting their wave nature.

However, we need to look more carefully at the output of the two detectors. Thanks to modern technology, we can measure the precise time of arrival of each of the sharp pulses. We find that a pulse is never registered by detector 2 at the same time as one registered by detector 3. In other words, the times of arrival of pulses at detector 2 never correlate with the times of arrival of pulses at detector 3. This implies that photons behave like particles, which do not split at the beam splitter but are equally likely to be reflected as transmitted. (Recall that, on average, we find equal numbers of reflection and transmission counts.) However, the photon capture rate is high, and it is possible that we are just missing the coincidences or that some other subtle effects are masking them.

Here is where we can appeal to the data in detector 1. The great value of the setup in figure 5.5 is that the photon pairs are perfectly correlated. To make use of this feature, we set the same distances from the photon source to each of the detectors. (This is not shown in figure 5.5, where the distance to detector 1 appears less than that to 2 or 3.) With this detector placement, we find that every pulse in detector 1 gives an identical detection at 2 or 3 but never at both 2 and 3 simultaneously. In other words, we never get triple coincidences at all detectors but only double coincidences at detector 1 and 2 or 1 and 3. With this arrangement, we know we are looking at *individual photons* and finding that half are transmitted while half are reflected, but *a single photon never splits.* With this data, photons seem to be acting just like extremely small ball bearings. A couple of decades ago such measurements were not possible. Now, thanks to modern technological advances and creative people like Galvez, we can perform measurements on individual photons in undergraduate laboratories. As we will see, single photon experiments illuminate important quantum properties in a particularly clear and powerful way.

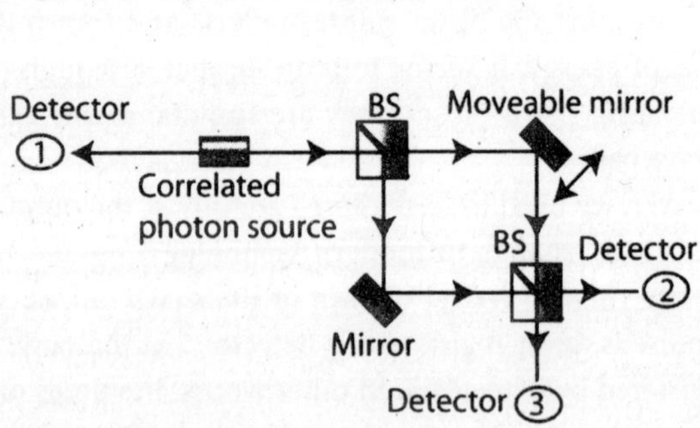

FIGURE 5.6 *Interferometer*

Having seen that photons behave like particles, now consider a convincing expression of their wave nature. Figure 5.6 shows an interferometer, with the same components as in the previous figure but with another beam splitter and two mirrors. The upper right mirror includes an exquisitely sensitive device that moves this mirror according to the voltage applied to it, as indicated by the double-headed arrow. Here the mirrors perfectly reflect the transmitted and reflected beams from the first beam splitter into the second beam splitter and then into detectors 2 and 3. Keep in mind that the beam splitter at the bottom right in the figure splits both the beam coming down and the beam moving from left to right.

Just as in the previous experiment, we never get triple coincidences in all three detectors, only coincidences in detectors 1 and 2 or in 1 and 3. However, something new happens with this setup. For now, forget about detector 3. Start by adjusting the moveable mirror so that both photon paths from the first beam splitter to the second one are of equal length. Then the perfect correlations between detectors 1 and 2 are at maximum strength. Next, apply a voltage to the moveable mirror so that paths between the beam splitters have different lengths and collect the number of perfect correlations or coincidences between detectors 1 and 2. Figure 5.7 shows the number of coincidences between detectors 1 and 2 found in twenty-second intervals as a function of the voltage applied to the moveable mirror. Kiko Galvez has calculated that we can be certain that only one photon is in the interferometer at a time. Therefore, the question arises: "What is giving rise to this nearly perfectly sinusoidal behavior of the coincidences shown in figure 5.7?"

Here is a beautiful example of wave superposition or wave interference (the terms are synonyms), the ability of waves to add according to the phase relationship between them. Let me illustrate interference by going back to the imaginary beach with the breakwater mentioned above. This time, get away from the breakwater, and just imagine two identical waves moving toward the same location but coming from different directions. Let the

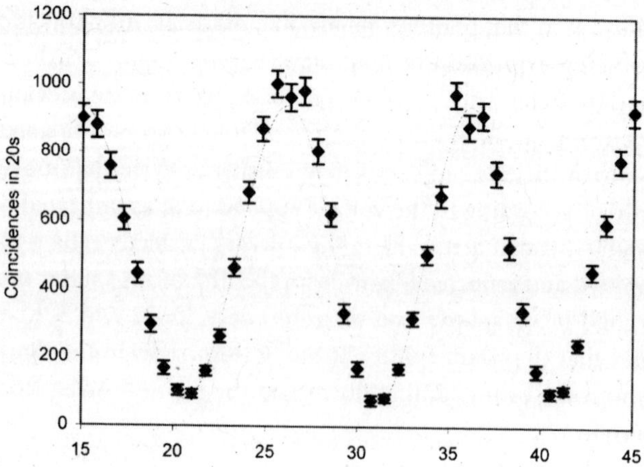

FIGURE 5.7. *Coincidences between detectors 1 and 2*

two waves with the same amplitude arrive at the specified location such that their crests arrive at the same time (completely in phase, like people marching in step). Then, the resulting wave is a superposition or interference of the two original waves to give a total wave that is twice the height of either original wave.

On the other hand, consider the case when the trough of one wave arrives just when the crest of another does. In this case, they are completely out of phase, like my leading the march with my right foot while you lead with your left. Then, at the point of their intersection, the waves superpose in cancellation, and the water is completely flat, without any disturbance. Of course, there are intermediate cases between these extremes. With a little careful observation at the beach, you can easily observe this hallmark feature of waves.

In the interferometer (figure 5.6), distinguish the path length for the beam reflected off the moveable mirror from the path length for the beam reflected off the fixed mirror. When these two path lengths are the same, the two beams enter the second beam splitter with the same phase, and we get constructive interference—in other words, they add. When the two path lengths differ by plus or minus half a wavelength of the light, then the two beams arrive at the second beam splitter exactly out of phase, and we get total destructive interference—they cancel each other out. More generally when the two path lengths differ by zero or some integer multiple of one wavelength, the waves arrive at the second beam splitter exactly in phase, and we get the peaks seen in figure 5.7. We get the minima in the figure when the path lengths differ by odd integer multiples of half a wavelength, so that the waves arrive completely out of phase.

Although photons clearly display particle properties, such as the sharp pulses detected, this superposition or interference phenomenon is clear and convincing evidence that they also act like waves. In all these experiments, we are certain that only one photon is in the system at a time. Although the photon always registers as a sharp pulse, as though coming from a single particle, it appears to be interfering with itself to give the interference pattern. But what could it mean for a particle to interfere with itself? Notice also that it takes the accumulation of many photon counts over several seconds to reveal their wave nature. Here we are approaching one of the central mysteries of quantum mechanics, which I will elaborate carefully.

We can go a bit deeper into this mysterious relationship between waves and particles by modifying the interferometer so that we can tell along which path the photon traveled in getting to detector 2. For what follows, we need not be concerned with detector 3. Imagine that we replaced the fixed mirror with one so delicately balanced that a single reflecting photon could jiggle it. Then, measuring when the jiggle takes place tells us which path the photon took in getting to detector 2. Of course, if detector 2 registers a count without a mirror jiggle, we know that the photon went along the other path. Knowing which path the photon took gives us particle information since a chief characteristic of particles is their having a well-defined trajectory. Now, while monitoring when the mirror jiggles and changing the path length differences by applying a voltage to the moveable mirror, we find we never get an interference pattern.

Experiments clearly show that, when we know which path the photon took (particle information), we never get an interference pattern (wave information).

The idea of a jiggling mirror (explained in the previous gray section) is conceptually simple but not technically feasible. However, there are many technically elegant ways of determining along which path the photon traveled. No matter what the method, *when we know path information, we never get an interference pattern.* More generally, when we know the particle nature of the photon, such as along which path it traveled, it never displays its wave nature, such as generating an interference pattern. Conversely, not knowing along which path the photon traveled, and thereby relinquishing knowledge of its particle nature, we see an interference pattern. This wave–particle behavior of the photon is an expression of the principle of complementarity, the very heart of quantum mechanics.

The above analysis is a good example of the complementarity discussed in the previous chapter. There I tried to give a visual analog of complementarity by showing the cube of lines that spontaneously flipped from one view or the other but never both at the same time. The important points to recall here are:

1. Complementary properties (such as waves and particles) require mutually exclusive experimental conditions for their study.
2. Both poles of a complementary pair are equally real and important in characterizing a quantum system.
3. A unitary reality encompasses all complementary properties in the form of possibilities for manifestation.

A Short Foray into Quantum Theory

So far, I have stayed close to the results of actual experiments in discussing the nature of photons. Let me briefly turn to some general features of quantum theory, which can answer the following question. Given that photons have a wave nature, what kind of wave is it? For example, in water waves, it is water undergoing wave motion, while sound waves consist of compression waves of air. But what is waving in quantum mechanics? To answer this important question, we must discuss a little mathematics, some of which you have already learned in school.

Start with the operation of taking the square root of a number. Taking the square root of a number gives a number whose square (the number multiplied by itself) returns the original number. For example, the square root of 100 is 10. The square of 10 (10 x 10) gives 100, the original number. Here is one more example, this time using the standard mathematical notation for the square root and the squaring operation. $(4)^{1/2} = 2$ and $2^2 = 4$. All this is probably at least vaguely familiar, and you may even recall learning an algorithm for taking square roots. Since even the simplest of calculators have square root functions, most of us have forgotten the algorithm a long time ago.

However, here is an interesting complication. What happens when you ask your simple calculator to take the square root of -1? If it is like the one that comes with the operating system on this computer, it will complain that you have invalid input to the function or something like that. Beginning in the sixteenth century, mathematicians introduce the idea of the complex number, i, where $i = (-1)^{1/2}$ so that $i^2 = -1$. It, therefore, obeys the properties of square roots. However, we do not meet with complex numbers in the course of our daily lives, whether in balancing our checkbook or doing carpentry. For this reason, René Descartes called these numbers *imaginary*, a derogatory term in contrast to real numbers. The term *imaginary number* stuck and is still widely used. Despite all my years of working with these numbers in all sorts of applications, they still have for me a bit of mystery about them.

Once you have i, all sorts of generalizations are possible. For example, $(-4)^{1/2} = 2i$ and $(2i)^2 = -4$. Now you can define a general complex number $N = a + ib$, where a and b are any real numbers that can be positive or negative. General complex numbers can be added, subtracted, multiplied, and divided, just like real numbers. I introduce them here because they play a pivotal role in quantum mechanics.

Recall that quantum theory only gives probabilities for the results of future measurements. We find these probabilities by forming the absolute square of the probability amplitude or wave function, which is a complex number like N defined above. (An "absolute square" is a more general squaring operation that can accommodate complex numbers. The absolute square of a complex number always gives a positive real number.) Let me say it in a little different way. You start with a wave function, a complex number. Then, take its absolute square to get a probability estimate for the results expected for future measurements. It may seem strange that you need the square root of minus one for quantum mechanics, but there is no way around it. Complex numbers are built into the theory at the deepest levels.

These probability amplitudes or wave functions have wave properties such as a wavelength and the ability to interfere. Although quantum theory tells us the probability of detecting a particle at a given point in three-dimensional space at a given time, the amplitudes themselves evolve in *Hilbert Space*, an abstract mathematical space. We only need to know two critical things about Hilbert Space. First, Hilbert Space is a complex space. Second, Hilbert Space has an infinite number of dimensions. Now, this second attribute presents serious problems. We can easily understand that the surface of this page is a two-dimensional space and that your body occupies a three-dimensional space. But how can we visualize even a four-dimensional space, let alone an infinite-dimensional, complex space? We cannot visualize such spaces. Although we can analyze such spaces with full generality using modern mathematics, there is simply no way to picture them.

Prior to an actual measurement event, all we can say is that the system is represented by probability amplitudes evolving in infinite-dimensional, complex Hilbert Space. We needed to discuss complex numbers and Hilbert Space to make it clear that these wave functions or probability amplitudes are not physical states in any reasonable sense of the term. Through taking the absolute square, we can turn these probability amplitudes into predictions about future detections.

Prior to the detection, the probability amplitudes or wave function does not contain matter or energy like a sound or water wave. This concept is a difficult idea without any analog in classical physics. Despite the clarity and precision of the mathematical description of probability amplitudes, *we can make no accurate mental pictures of states prior to measurement*. Nevertheless, we are clear that the waves in quantum mechanics are *nonmaterial probability amplitudes*, whose absolute square gives the likelihood or probability of measuring a particle at that time and place. For example, consider the case when the probability amplitudes are large at a certain time and place. That situation implies that, if a measurement were made then, it is likely that a particle will be found at that time and place.

Since there are many references to probability in this chapter, a little discussion about them is in order. I want to draw a distinction between probabilities as expressing ignorance of an objective fact versus probabilities as describing objective indeterminacy. Probability as expressing ignorance of an objective fact occurs in classical or Newtonian physics and common speech. Probability as describing objective indeterminacy occurs in quantum mechanics in a genuinely new and important way.

Consider a simple example. I leave my office to teach class. I cannot recall whether I turned off my office light when leaving the room. I estimate that the probability of the light being on in my office is 1/3. Of course, the probability that the light is off is 2/3. Here probability is a measure of my *ignorance of an objective condition*: whether the light is actually on or off. Anybody could go to my office and examine the state of the light, but their examining the light would not change its state.

In contrast, probability in quantum mechanics does not express ignorance of an objective condition. Rather, the theory only gives probability estimates for the results of potential measurement outcomes. For example, when the theory says that the probability of the photon being measured at a certain time and place is 1/3, it is not referring to an objective matter of fact but only what to expect in a future measurement. *There is no objective state with well-defined properties prior to a measurement. Before a measurement, nature is objectively indeterminate, in a state of pure potentiality.* This means that, if I had a quantum mechanical office with a quantum mechanical light in it, prior to measurement, it would be in a superposition or interference state of the light being both on and off. At this point, neither state actually exists in any definite sense, but both light on and off are potential outcomes of measurement. Checking the state of the quantum office light (making a measurement), then, reveals one of the possible states (light on or off) with the appropriate likelihoods for each option.

The only way I could check the validity of the quantum description of my office would be to prepare a very large number of identical offices in the same state (1/3 light on). I then measure each identical office and find that some have a light on and some have it off. When I measure enough of them, however, the results converge accurately to 1/3 with light on. I hope you see that this is not using probability as expressing ignorance of an objective fact but instead expresses an *objective indeterminacy or randomness* at the heart of quantum mechanics. This objective indeterminacy at the heart of quantum mechanics is a radically new feature. It is arguably quantum theory's most important contribution to our understanding of the world.

This point about probability's being an expression of the underlying indeterminacy of nature is so important that I will provide another clarifying example. When I presented some of these ideas about the role of probability in quantum mechanics at the Sambosa Diamond Meditation Center in Carmel, California, the first Korean monastery in America, a woman friend asked why it was any different from the way probability is used in medicine. For example, let's say that there is a large population of heavy cigarette smokers and that we know that, after twenty years there is a certain probability, call it PC, that a given smoker will have lung cancer. We cannot say for any given smoker whether she will get lung cancer, but we can make probability estimates. So far, this sounds like the quantum mechanical case.

However, there is a major difference. Whether a person ends up with lung cancer does not depend upon any measurement or diagnosis. We do not believe that the doctor's diagnosis precipitates the disease (if so, she would get very few patients!) but rather reveals the underlying cancer that already existed prior to the examination in an unknown but objective state. *In other words, a diagnosis or set of measurements on a patient reveals an objective matter of fact that existed prior to the diagnosis. In contrast, in quantum mechanics a measurement actually brings about a transformation from an evolving superposition of probabilities that do not exist in physical space-time into an actual space-time event.* In the medical case, the probabilities are expressions of ignorance, not expressions of the underlying indeterminacy of nature as they are in quantum mechanics. In addition, prior to their manifestation, the quantum probabilities interfere just like waves. These interference effects give rise to well-studied consequences. The medical case does not seem to have any such interference effects resulting from superposition of probability amplitudes.

However, there is a complicating point. It may be that whether a person gets cancer or not depends upon quantum processes in cells. These processes may be biased one way or another depending upon health habits such as smoking, exercise, and diet. Then, it may be that a superposition of quantum states is at the heart of who gets cancer and who does not. It is possible that, when microbiologists investigate more deeply the genesis of disease, they will find that quantum mechanics plays an important role. However, for the present, my point above still holds: the use of probabilities in medicine is an expression of ignorance of objective details, not of the fundamental indeterminacy of nature.

As we saw in discussing the interferometer, probability amplitudes interfere, just like water waves. However, as I have been stressing, although probability amplitudes interfere and have a wavelength, they are not physical or material like other waves. We should also keep in mind that standard quantum mechanics is by far the best theory in the history of physics. Nothing is even remotely in the same class. Of course, like all theories in physics, it is subject to change and improvements. Nevertheless, the central feature of probability amplitudes or wave functions evolving in Hilbert Space prior to a measurement has been with us for eight decades, since quantum mechanics was first given its current mathematical formulation. All attempts to replace it by a theory that seems more physically plausible have failed. Although the current attempts at unifying the four forces of nature in some grand unification scheme have not been successful so far, to the best of my knowledge, none of them seeks to replace this feature of standard quantum mechanics. Of course, this does not guarantee that quantum mechanics will always have its present form, but it is what we have now and what I will work with in the rest of this chapter.

The task in quantum mechanics is, given the details of the system, to solve the dynamical equations that tell how these probability amplitudes evolve in time and thereby predict the possible outcomes of experiments. For example, we can find probability amplitudes or wave functions for photons traveling along the two arms of the interferometer. Knowing how these probability amplitudes interfere, we can then predict the likelihood of photon detections. The accumulation of photon counts with time reveals the underlying interference pattern of the probability amplitudes.

In contrast, to understand how ball bearings move through space in the experiment that started this chapter, we appeal to Newton's dynamical and gravitational laws. These laws are completely causal: given the forces on a ball bearing and its starting conditions, we can predict exactly the state of the ball at any later time. Then Newtonian physics gives a detailed path or trajectory of exactly how the ball moves through the air.

Returning to quantum mechanics, it is important to appreciate that there are two distinct forms of evolution, only one of which is truly mysterious. First, there is a continuous and causal evolution of the nonphysical probability amplitudes between the time when the system is prepared and the time it is measured. This causal evolution in Hilbert Space, governed by quantum mechanical equations, means that, given the state of the probability amplitudes at one time, we can predict with certainty exactly what these amplitudes will be at another time. This is completely analogous to specifying the state of the surface waves at any one time in your coffee cup and using the equation for surface waves to find the exact state of the waves at any other time.

However, probability amplitudes are not physical waves in three-dimensional space like water waves; they evolve in infinite dimensional, complex Hilbert Space. Their causal evolution accounts for the continuity of the quantum system without positing any independently existing material entity, no inherently existing photon moving through the system apparatus. It therefore bears a striking resemblance to the Middle Way continuity of causality through disintegratedness. We could accurately say that, at each moment of the evolution of the quantum probabilities, they are undergoing production, abiding, and disintegration, which continuously gives rise to another moment of production, abiding, and disintegration—all without any underlying material entity, just as in Middle Way disintegratedness.

Second, a measurement disrupts this causal quantum evolution in a completely unpredictable way to reveal a particular outcome. In this context, measurement means the irreversible registration of some physical effect, such as a pulse in a detector. It is irreversible since a pulse never disappears by changing itself back into a photon. This so-called measurement-induced "collapse" of the probability amplitude or wave function is the point where the noncausal or probabilistic element enters quantum mechanics. Here is the heart of the mystery where the theory can only make probability estimates for possible outcomes but never say exactly which outcome will occur nor give any details about the collapse process. (In honor of the Middle Way, we could equally well call it a disintegration process, with the resulting state being one of disintegratedness.) For convenience, I refer to the causal evolution of the probability amplitudes as Type I evolution and to the noncausal collapse or disintegration to a particular result as Type II evolution. We know from both theory and experiment that the transition from probability amplitudes to measured events is instantaneous. In other words, the collapse from possibilities to actualities takes no time. Figure 5.8 summarizes these two types of evolution.

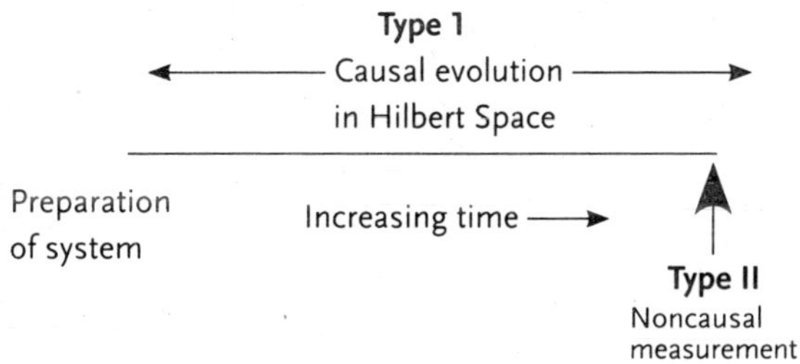

FIGURE 5.8. *Two types of quantum evolution*

Between the creation of the correlated photon pairs (preparation of the system) and just prior to the actual measurement, we have only Type I evolution in Hilbert Space. During this time, there is neither a trajectory nor any physical entity that continuously traces out a path in space and time. Largely because it is so alien to our everyday experience, it is difficult for both students and experts alike to appreciate that, *in quantum mechanics, there is no material or energetic entity continuously tracing out a well-defined trajectory in space.* Here we have a fundamental expression of continuity without any inherent identity. In a measurement, or in Type II evolution, there is an instantaneous transition from these ethereal possibilities or potentialities in Hilbert Space to actual manifest events such as a pulse in a detector. Prior to measurement, there is never anything to grab onto as if it were a tiny ball bearing; yet the existence of our bodies, the world, and the sight of our beloved are dependent upon both Type I and Type II evolution.

We verify the correctness of quantum mechanics by making many measurements (accumulating many detector counts) and comparing their distribution (for example, figure 5.7) to the theoretical predictions. Although there is no doubt about its predictive accuracy, there are still vexing fundamental questions about what it means for our view of the physical universe. The recent single photon experiments discussed above make it possible to demonstrate several deep truths and mysteries of quantum mechanics in a dramatic and convincing fashion. Now, I turn to addressing how quantum mechanical theory relates to the Tibetan Buddhist understanding of substantial causes and cooperative conditions.

Photons, Causes, and Conditions

Quantum mechanics' most significant departures from Newtonian and Middle Way causality occur in Type II evolution—the instantaneous transition from probability amplitudes to an actual measurement event. Since Type I causal evolution presents no problems, I will focus on Type II.

Consider the detection of a single photon in a detector, the registration of a sharp pulse from a particular photon. Since Type II evolution always involves an *instantaneous* transformation from probability amplitudes in Hilbert Space to actual measured entities in conventional time and space, there can be *no direct substantial cause for the detection of a given photon*. There is no "continuum of a similar type" that is required for all substantial causes. The state of the system as a mere potentiality in Hilbert Space is discontinuous with the actual measurement event in conventional time and space. Are there *indirect substantial causes* for the photon detection? No: because of the discontinuity of type or nature between the probability amplitudes in Hilbert Space and the detected photon, there cannot be any indirect or direct substantial causes for a particular photon detection.

Are there *cooperative conditions or contributing causes* for the detection of a particular photon? As I stressed throughout this chapter, whenever there is more than one possible outcome of a measurement, quantum theory can only provide probabilities for measurement outcomes. It can never say with certainty which outcome will occur in a Type II evolution. In other words, *there are no quantum mechanical causes for individual measurements*. Thus, there are no direct cooperative conditions or contributing causes for a particular measurement.

Are there *indirect cooperative conditions*? Recall that Type I evolution has both direct and indirect substantial causes and cooperative conditions. It is therefore true that earlier moments of Type I evolution, along with the dynamical equations of quantum mechanics, provide substantial causes and contributing conditions for later states of Type I. However, since quantum theory cannot provide *any* distinct causes for an individual measurement event, there can be no indirect cooperative conditions or contributing causes for a particular measurement. In short, when we consider a unique measurement, it has no direct or indirect substantial causes or cooperative conditions. The physics community, to my knowledge, has never employed the Tibetan Buddhist categories of causality in analyzing Type II evolution. However, doing so clearly reveals the radical lack of causality for individual events at the heart of quantum mechanics.

Summary and Some Implications

The second Noble Truth speaks about the cause of suffering, while the fourth Noble Truth tells us how to use causality to eliminate suffering. As we know from chapter 3, causality is one of the primary arguments used to establish emptiness, the philosophic heart of Buddhism and the foundation for enlightenment and the cultivation of limitless compassion.

The Middle Way view of causality is so compatible with classical or Newtonian physics that I used an example from Newtonian physics to review direct and indirect substantial causes and cooperative conditions. However, there are significant differences between Middle Way causality and quantum mechanical Type II evolution for individual events. There is no substance, no entity with a well-defined type or nature, persisting through Type II evolution. Therefore, the instantaneous collapse of the interfering probability amplitudes in Hilbert Space to a particular event in empirical space-time has neither direct nor indirect substantial causes. When considering an individual event in Type II evolution, there are also no direct or indirect cooperative conditions.

At the level of individual events, quantum mechanical causality diverges from the Middle Way understanding. Although the analysis of Type II evolution using Middle Way understanding of causality clarifies some philosophic issues, it does not point the way toward the resolution of any vexing quantum mechanical problems.

Given the dominance of science and its relative insensitivity to outside influences, it is highly unlikely that the divergence between Middle Way causality and quantum physics will challenge physics. However, we can ask if this divergence challenges Buddhism. The Dalai Lama has said that, if science definitely proves a Buddhist tenet wrong, then Buddhism must change. For example, he says, "Buddhists believe in rebirth. But suppose that through various investigative means, science one day comes to the definite conclusion that there is no rebirth. If this is definitively proven, then we must accept it and we will accept it. This is the general Buddhist idea."[10] Within this attitude, the question naturally arises, "Does the lack of causality in quantum mechanics have significant implications for Buddhism?"

Let me begin answering this question by noting that the divergent views on causality between quantum mechanics and the Middle Way do not deny Buddhist arguments for emptiness. In fact, appreciating Type I evolution as continuous transformation of probability amplitudes or wave functions without any underlying physical entity only strengthens the case for emptiness, the lack of independent existence. This is also true for Type II evolution, the instantaneous transformation of potentialities into actualities. Besides not being able to predict which possible outcome will be actualized, the dependency of any outcome on the very act of measurement confirms the lack of independent existence of quantum entities, whether elementary particles in isolation or in entangled pairs, as in the previous chapter. Thus, the case for emptiness is strengthened, but other parts of Buddhism may be challenged.

Since Buddhism understands causality as central to understanding both the source and elimination of suffering, if quantum mechanics effectively challenges the rule of causality, this could shake the very deepest foundation of Buddhism. Perhaps this is the reason for the concern expressed by the Dalai Lama and the *geshes* at Namgyal about the lack of causality in quantum mechanics. Here I briefly consider one possible implication for Buddhism of the breakdown of causality in quantum mechanics and the brain. I will then return to the question of Darwinian evolution.

A. Quantum Mechanics and the Brain

The brain is perhaps the most complicated structure known. Although individual quantum events undoubtedly occur in the brain, it is still a subject of research and debate whether such individual events are important for brain functioning that correlates with mental activity. It is possible that individual quantum events have no significant role in mental activity. Then, given the primary Buddhist goal of relieving suffering, they can largely neglect quantum mechanics when considering mental activity. On the other hand, if, as many believe, individual quantum events are crucial for brain functioning that correlates to mental states, then quantum mechanics could directly affect Buddhism. Notice that to claim that mental states *correlate* with brain states does not necessarily imply a *causal* relationship, let alone a relation of *equivalence*, which claims that mental states are reducible to brain states. Therefore, to consider such correlations does not bind us to a reductive materialist approach to consciousness.

The role of quantum mechanics in consciousness is a highly technical topic that is still in the early developmental stage. (The *Stanford Encyclopedia of Philosophy* provides an excellent up-to-date overview, which assumes a quantum mechanics background.[11]) Current theories are neither sufficiently developed nor verified experimentally. However, if there is genuine randomness in the physical states of the brain that correlate with mental states, then this has implications for morality. For example, consider the case where a significant moral act has a strong correlation to a single quantum event with its irreducible randomness. The tight correlation might mean that my individual morally significant acts have an irreducible randomness about them. For example, I could sincerely intend a morally positive act but might randomly generate evil, despite my genuinely good intentions. Nevertheless, when looked at in large groups, moral acts should have well-defined statistical averages. Judging from common experience, when we intend morally positive acts, they generally occur. Yet, this is not always the case. As St. Paul lamented in Romans 7:19, "For the good that I want, I do not do, but I practice the very evil that I do not want." Can St. Paul and the rest of us be rescued by claiming, "That inevitably probabilistic Type II evolution ruined me again!" Is it enough for Buddhism to say that, although individual acts may not be causally determined, as a group they are bound by well-defined statistical averages? I cannot answer these questions, but their seriousness for Buddhism is obvious.

In this one example, we can see the possible relevance of Type II evolution on Buddhist spiritual practice and theory. Although discussing the single photon experiments in this chapter reveals some strange quantum phenomena, they may have great relevance even for the monk in a long meditation retreat in a remote cave.

I do not believe, however, that science alone can answer the question of the relevance of quantum mechanics for consciousness. Throughout its history, science has developed through systematically removing all references to the subject. Therefore, in its present form, I believe that science cannot explain consciousness with its irreducible subjective aspect. On the other hand, although Buddhism has developed extraordinary technology for studying the subjective, on its own it does not have the ability to study scientifically the enormous complexities of the brain and its influence upon our behavior. However, a partnership between the scientific laboratory and the monk in a cave could understand consciousness in more profound ways than either of them could separately. Such a partnership could then make significant contributions to the relief of suffering.

Unfortunately, not everybody shares my enthusiasm for a partnership between Buddhism and science. The Society for Neuroscience 2005 convention asked the Dalai Lama to be a keynote speaker and discuss the measurements that have been made of the brains of advanced practitioners of meditation.[12] This aroused Dr. Jianguo Gu to submit a petition to the Society protesting the invitation, claiming that it was bad science to involve a religious leader in a scientific meeting. As can easily be seen, almost all those signing the Gu's petition are Chinese scientists.[13] Has politics polluted science?

B. Returning to Darwin

Recall the two-step process of evolution that consists of random mutations and natural selection. These random mutations are governed by Type II evolution. It is, therefore, completely random in the deepest sense of the term whether these mutations are positive, neutral, or negative in the sense of their reproductive success. Thus, there can be no purpose, endpoint, or teleology in Darwinian evolution. In fact, if you could wind the clock back by three billion years or so and let the whole system evolve again, very different life-forms would result. Because the process is so extraordinarily complex with its innumerable branchings, it is not even possible to answer the question of how similar these imagined life-forms might be to present life-forms. This little thought experiment of winding the clock back and letting the process restart reveals how deeply meaningless or purposeless a strictly Darwinian evolution is.

It is obvious that this has serious implications for Buddhism or, for that matter, any religious point of view. Nevertheless, I want to connect it more intimately to Buddhism by telling a little story. One day my wife and I were walking in the woods with our dog. Suddenly, we came upon a new partridge nest right in the middle of the path. Partridges always build their nests on the forest floor, but this seemed like a particularly inappropriate place for it. As soon as the partridge noticed our dog, it ran off on the ground through the woods. It had a very badly broken wing and limped clumsily as it tore through the underbrush. Our big black lab instantly gave chase and totally ignored our appeals to stop. Just as the dog appeared to be closing in on the wounded partridge, it gracefully flew up into a tree. Its wing was fine! By then the dog had completely forgotten about the nest and was in a great frenzy about the tasty bird that it just missed. We examined the nest and found it had a beautiful clutch of eggs.

The partridge purposely lured our dog away from the vulnerable eggs with its feigned injury. This is a common trick of partridges. What a beautiful piece of adaptation for a bird that builds its nests on the ground! I thought of how mothers of all species protect their young through strategies both blunt and subtle. I reminisced lovingly of how my own mother protected me. However, if we believe Darwin, a mother's protection is just biological evolution and has nothing to do with love in any exalted sense of the term. Rather, those mothers who did not defend their offspring with their lives simply did not compete well and lost out in the natural selection race. So when the Buddhists extol a mother's love so movingly and ask us to use it as a means for developing universal compassion,[14] what does that mean? Are we just praising the meaningless product of random mutations and natural selection? What about all the suffering of those early partridges who had not yet learned how to be good decoys?

For a rigorous Darwinist, there is nothing special about suffering, despite its centrality in the Four Noble Truths. The way life has evolved on our planet, only organisms with sufficiently evolved nervous systems can survive. Such nervous systems inevitably bring suffering as the price of reproductive success. We survive because we naturally flee from pain as an important part of our adaptation to this planet. For a strict Darwinist, it makes little sense to focus as the Buddhists do on suffering, its causes, elimination, transformative potentials, and so forth.

Of course, many people, the Dalai Lama included, find this perspective unacceptable. We believe that love and suffering are deep truths of spiritual life, that they are pivots around which our moral actions turn. Furthermore, we have the intuitive sense that our life is meaningful, that it has a purpose beyond the mere reproductive success of our offspring. For some Christians, this discomfort compels them to invoke the idea that God guides evolution. This creationism, or in its more modern guise, Intelligent Design, is no longer science because it evokes a supernatural agent. I am sympathetic to the plight of everyone from the Dalai Lama to the Christian fundamentalists who find Darwinian evolution troubling because of its lack of purpose, but this is the clear implication of strict Darwinian evolution. In fact, such meaninglessness and its devaluing of love and suffering trouble me deeply. I believe that life is meaningful, yet I do not doubt the lack of causality in quantum physics and its direct expression in Darwinian evolution. I do not know how to resolve this tension. However, I know that to impose scriptural ideas upon science is not the solution. My only hope is that holding this tension with intensity and integrity will allow some synthetic and satisfying point of view to arise, but there is no guarantee that such a view will come to pass.

Of course, if you invoke nonphysical causes, whether *karma*, disintegratedness, or creationism, this picture changes drastically. However, when you leave the physically measurable realm, you leave science and give up on any Buddhism and science dialogue or collaboration.

I turn to one last application of random mutation and evolution: the avian influenza or bird flu currently propagating around our globe. Viruses are particularly fragile structures and, therefore, mutate easily. This mutability is the reason you need a new flu shot every year. The picture in figure 5.9 below, provided by the United States Center for Disease Control,[15] shows the avian influenza virus, H5N1. In this colorized microscope image, the influenza virus appears as dark rods, which when seen end on end appear as small, dark, circular structures. The virus is growing in cells, which appear as lighter colored more amorphous structures. Recent gene sequencing[16] shows the close similarity of H5N1 to the virus that caused the 1918 pandemic that killed approximately fifty million people. This means approximately twenty-five mutations could turn H5N1 into an influenza that is very similar to that which caused the 1918 pandemic. Exactly which genes need to change for it to become easily transmissible between humans and a lethal virus are still subjects of research. The point is that so few changes need to occur. Of course, these changes being truly random, we have no way to predict accurately the likelihood of this outcome. All we can be sure of is that those changes making the virus more likely to spread are favored by natural selection and that random mutations are always generating new candidates for the natural selection process. Many experts believe that, given enough time, it is inevitable that a pandemic like the 1918 version will arise, if not from H5N1 then from some other virus.

Because of the truly random nature of the Type II evolution that generates the mutations, we cannot ascribe any meaning or purpose to these mutations and the possible pandemic that might arise. The point is that, contrary to Buddhist views, which assert the primacy of causality and its

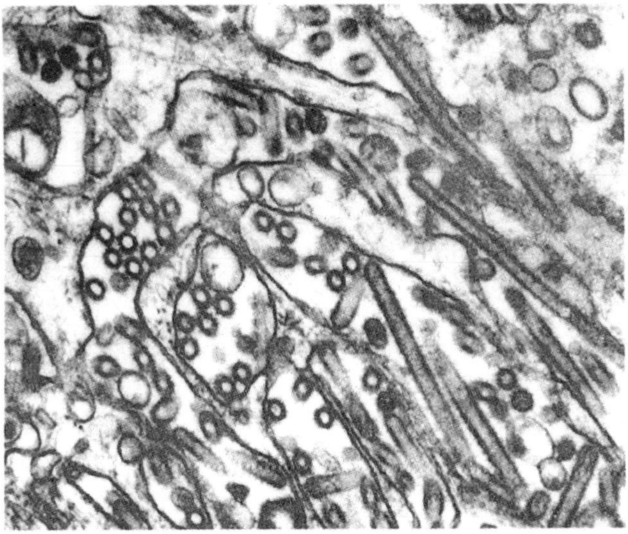

FIGURE 5.9. *Avian influenza among cells*
(Courtesy of C. Goldsmith, J. Katz, and S. Zaki, U.S. Center for Disease Control)

expression of nonphysical karmic forces, modern genetics tells us that whether you live or die from a possible pandemic is a completely random act. For me, this drives home the conflict between Type II evolution and the Buddhist understanding of causality (including nonphysical factors) in a very personal way.

It is also easy to see how Buddhists would contend that restricting yourself to just physical causes would never yield a satisfactory explanation of evolution. At the same time, as science is presently constituted, there is no way to study nonphysical factors systematically in the laboratory. If this conflict between Buddhism and science is to be resolved, it will require at least a significant broadening of what is usually meant by experiment. Perhaps as Alan Wallace and others have suggested, we need to find precise and exacting ways of incorporating first-person, subjective accounts into scientific experiments.[17]

6: Rel

INTRO

F

me focu

good u

suspend

held in

easier t

Lately

premis

good he

ending

one mi

will gra

lecturin

longing

somethi

Th

In th

Head

approa

tempo

6. Relativity and the Arrow of Time

Introduction

Here I sit in a cramped seat in an intercontinental economy class flight. Despite the discomfort, I love flying. For long stretches of time, I am alone with my thoughts. The increased airport security and recent history of commercial flight keep me focused on the impermanence and fragility of life. Although I have a good understanding of the physical laws of flight, it is still a miracle to be suspended in the air above the jeweled mountains of Scandinavia. Being held in the sky by a delicate network of impermanence makes it much easier to contemplate the great truths of Buddhism.

Lately impermanence and the preciousness of life have been especially prominent in my mind. This spring, I turned sixty-five. Even with my good health, an inner voice incessantly urges me to realize that my life is ending. Although I find great satisfaction in teaching, I am retiring after one more year. After so many decades of watching students graduate, I will graduate to a more concentrated period of meditation, writing, and lecturing. Along with the sobering realization of my advanced age, I am longing for the new opportunities. The author Jorge Luis Borges captures something of my feelings:

> Time is the substance I am made of. Time is a river which sweeps me along, but I am the river; it is a tiger that devours me, but I am the tiger; it is a fire that consumes me, but I am the fire.[1]

In this chapter, I significantly expand and refine a chapter in my book *Head and Heart: A Personal Exploration of Science and the Sacred* by approaching time and impermanence from two directions.[2] First, we temporarily set aside our discussion of quantum mechanics and turn to relativity—the other great theory forming the heart of modern physics. Each theory has revolutionized our view of the world, and my discussion of the essence of time within Einstein's special relativity will show relativity's intimate connections with the Middle Way. The second direction discusses the "arrow of time," that there is directionality in time, that the past is qualitatively different from the future. For example, although I have almost no regrets, there are a few things I would like to change in the past, but I clearly cannot do so. Yes, I could change my understanding or interpretation of the past, but the past has a clear fixity that contrasts with the malleability of the future, with its possibility for transformation and change.

Space is different. The space behind me is qualitatively the same as the space in front of me, while the events behind me (in the past) are qualitatively different from the events in front of me (in the future). The different natures of space and time suggest that time has a direction, that there is an "arrow of time." This is a particularly interesting problem in modern physics. It engages us in a combination of modern thermodynamics and cosmology and displays some extraordinary connections to the Middle Way. Finally, I hope to provide some amplification of the idea that time "is a fire that consumes me, but I am the fire."

Relativity in Physics and the Middle Way

I love introducing beginning students to special relativity. Only algebra is required and the ideas are elegantly simple, yet the consequences of the theory are so extraordinary and counterintuitive. Everything is deduced from one definition and two simple axioms.

Let's first clarify the definition of an inertial reference frame, one in which objects free of external forces maintain a constant velocity. Imagine a spaceship gliding silently through the dark vastness of intergalactic space far from any galaxies. Your shipmate asks you to pass the salt. You send the saltshaker toward her by setting it in motion in the appropriate direction and letting it go. The saltshaker glides with constant velocity toward her because it has no external forces on it and is in an inertial reference frame—the spaceship.

If the spaceship's rockets were suddenly turned on and the ship accelerated, it would no longer be an inertial reference frame. For accelerations at an angle to the saltshaker's velocity, the saltshaker once set free would follow a curved path (since its velocity would be changing relative to the spaceship) and might even hit a cabin wall before getting to your shipmate. For accelerations in the same direction as the velocity of the saltshaker, its velocity relative to the cabin would change. Thus, for any angle of the acceleration, the spaceship would no longer be an inertial reference frame.

The earth is not an inertial reference frame since free objects fall to the ground because of gravity. However, imagine an elevator whose cable has been cut. The elevator's acceleration due to gravity cancels the gravitational force, and the freely falling elevator becomes an inertial reference frame, one in which saltshakers would glide with constant velocity.

There are many easier ways to cancel the effects of gravity on earth and obtain an inertial reference frame. Imagine a smooth object gliding on ice. The upward force of the ice on the object cancels the gravitational force. Then, if we can neglect the small residual friction, the surface of the ice is an inertial reference frame. Frictionless pucks would glide with constant velocity. Actually, depending upon the experiment, we can often consider the surface of the earth or the body of this airplane to be an inertial reference frame. For example, if I am rolling frictionless ball bearings on the smooth floor of the airplane or my desk in my Colgate office, I can consider both the airplane and the desk as inertial reference frames.

The lovely thing about inertial reference frames is that, once you find one, you can find infinitely many others. Just set any reference frame into constant motion relative to the first frame, and you have another inertial reference frame. In summary, an inertial reference frame is one in which objects free of external forces move with constant velocity. There are infinitely many such frames, and special relativity restricts itself to just these reference frames. To break out of this restriction requires general relativity, which includes acceleration and gravity.

Now I turn to the two axioms upon which all of special relativity is built.

Axiom One

The speed of light, c, is a constant in any inertial reference frame, regardless of the motion of the source or the observer. This is simple enough, but it differs drastically from our ordinary experience. For example, say I shot a bullet, with a muzzle velocity, V_b, out of the front of this airplane. (A muzzle velocity is relative to the muzzle of the gun, or in this case, relative to the body of the airplane.) Let the velocity of the airplane relative to the ground be V_a. Then the velocity of the bullet relative to the ground is the sum of the velocities, $V_a + V_b$.

Here is another example. Imagine you are driving down the road in your car with a velocity of V_c relative to the ground. You throw a stone out of the car in the direction of travel with velocity of V_s. Then the velocity of the stone relative to the ground is $V_c + V_s$.

In contrast, if I shine a light out of the front of this airplane with velocity c with respect to the body of the airplane then, according to axiom one, the velocity of the light relative to the ground is still c, independent of the airplane velocity. Even if another airplane is approaching mine and the other airplane measures the velocity of the light I direct out of the front of this airplane, axiom one says they will still measure a velocity of c. I hope you see that this behavior is a long way from our ordinary experiences of how velocities add.

Does axiom one conflict with the lack of independent existence of all phenomena, both objective and subjective, in the Middle Way? In other words, is the velocity of light, c, some independently existent velocity? No: the velocity of anything, from bullets to electromagnetic energy or light, is defined in relation to some observer; it must be at least potentially measurable in some reference frame, so velocity is not independently or inherently existent.

Let me say this in another way. Imagine a single photon or a particle in a universe with absolutely nothing in it—just pure empty space and one particle. Is it possible to speak about the velocity or position of such an imaginary particle? No: to discuss velocity, we would need at least one other particle so that we can speak about the distance between them and their velocity relative to each other. There is no way of speaking about the position or velocity of a totally independent particle. Therefore, there is complete harmony between the Middle Way and axiom one.

Axiom Two

The laws of physics take the same form in any inertial reference frame. The laws of classical or Newtonian mechanics, quantum mechanics, electromagnetic theory, and so forth all take the same mathematical form in any inertial frame. In other words, all the fundamental equations of physics have the same mathematical structure in all inertial reference frames. (General relativity makes it possible for us to write the laws of physics in a form that is the same for all possible reference frames, but we need not be concerned with this level of generality.)

We actually have a great deal of first-hand experience with axiom two. Walking on the earth feels no different from walking on the airplane. The mechanics of walking are the same because the laws of mechanics take the same form in any inertial reference frame. Of course, if the airplane hits turbulence or is accelerating in takeoff, then walking is a very different experience. In the same way, our digital music player works the same on the ground as it does in the airplane because the laws of electromagnetism and quantum mechanics take the same form in any inertial reference frame.

With the definition of an inertial reference frame and the two axioms, we can derive all of special relativity using only algebra. In the next few paragraphs, I will derive the famous time dilation formula. This result destroys any notion we had of an independently existent time interval and echoes a result that has been a cornerstone of the Middle Way for many centuries. The derivation below with a gray background shows the kind of elegant reasoning that characterizes special relativity. Although I encourage you to look it over to at least get the flavor of the reasoning, it can be skipped if you are only interested in the conclusions.

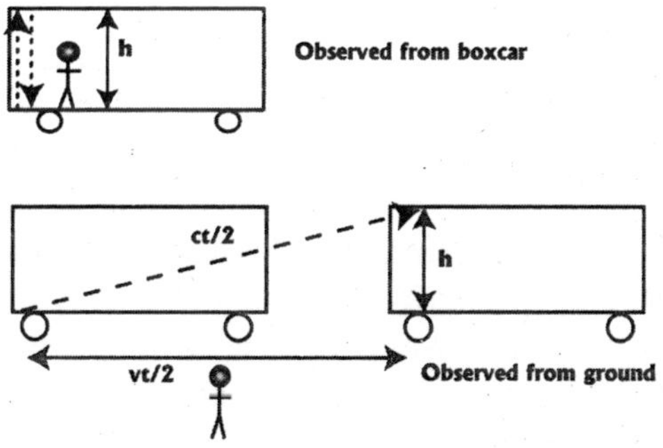

FIGURE 6.1. *Observing light clocks*

The following derivation is typically the first piece of special relativity presented in standard treatments of the subject. It begins by defining a special light clock. Consider the boxcar shown in the top of figure 6.1. Observed from the boxcar (by the top stick figure), a light signal starts upward from the floor, is reflected off the roof, and returns to its starting point. (I always show the trajectory of light as dashed lines.) The length of time this takes is then defined as one tick on the clock. If, as the diagram shows, the car has height h, then the time interval or the tick must be given by $t_0 = 2h/c$. We need the factor of two because the light traveled up a distance h and then down the same distance. The subscript 0 on the time interval denotes that it was measured by an observer in the boxcar who is at rest with respect to the light clock.

TABLE 6.1: SYMBOL ASSIGNMENTS

c = velocity of light

v = velocity of boxcar relative to tracks

h = boxcar height

t_0 = time for stationary observer (in the boxcar)

t = time for observer with velocity v relative to clock

TABLE 6.1. *Symbol assignments*

The bottom of figure 6.1 shows the situation for an observer who is stationary with respect to the tracks (the bottom stick figure). She sees the train move to the right with constant velocity v. Put glass sides on the boxcar to make it easier for her to observe the light clock. In this reference frame, during the time it takes for the light to reach the ceiling, the boxcar moves a distance vt/2 to the right. Notice that I have omitted the subscript 0 because this time interval is measured by the observer at rest with respect to the track. For that observer, the light clock has velocity v. In relativity, we must always specify the frame in which a quantity is measured. Without a specification of the reference frame, measurements are meaningless. Notice that I am using t/2 because the light signal has just gone to the roof of the boxcar and not the full round trip.

The distance that the light traveled is just ct/2 since we know that the speed of light is always c for any inertial frame. Then, we can use the Pythagorean formula to write:

$$(ct/2)^2 = (vt/2)^2 + h^2$$

With the definition $h = ct_0/2$ and a little bit of algebra, we find the famous time dilation formula:

$$t = \frac{t_0}{\sqrt{1 - \left(\frac{v}{c}\right)^2}}.$$

This relationship, the most radical conclusion of special relativity, says that the time as measured by an observer in the boxcar, t_0, is not the same time interval as that measured by an observer beside the track, for which the light clock has velocity v. Time runs slower for the observer beside the tracks. The closer v comes to c, the larger the deviation between t and t_0. To get a feeling for how t and t_0 vary with v, figure 6.2 plots t/t_0 versus v/c.

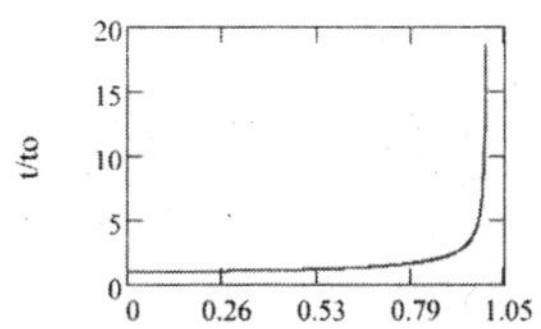

FIGURE 6.2

When v/c ~ 0.1, figure 6.2 shows that there is little difference between t and t_0. However, when v/c > 0.8 the ratio t/t_0 starts changing drastically. Of course, boxcars or even high-speed jets cannot travel a significant fraction of c. However, elementary particles routinely travel this fast, and the time dilation formula has been confirmed innumerable times by a wide variety of experiments.

$$t = \frac{t_0}{\sqrt{1-\left(\frac{v}{c}\right)^2}}.$$

FIGURE 6.3

I restate the time dilation formula in figure 6.3, where t_0 is the time interval or clock tick as measured by an observer at rest with respect to the clock. Time t is the time interval as measured by an observer that sees the clock moving with velocity v. This relationship, the most fundamental conclusion in special relativity, says that moving clocks run slower compared to stationary clocks. In the grayed-out paragraph below, I work a specific example, which you can enjoy or skip depending upon your taste.

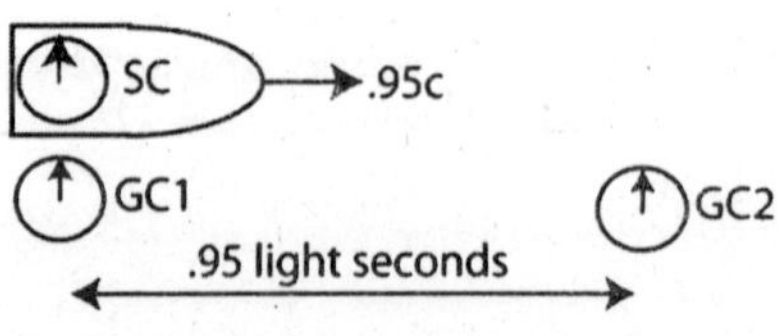

FIGURE 6.4. *Spaceship and clocks*

Here is a specific example. You and I have identical clocks, and you pass me in a spaceship with velocity of 0.95c. Let's call your clock on the spaceship SC (for spaceship clock), while my clock is labeled GC1, for ground clock 1. When you pass me, both our clocks SC and GC1 read zero. As shown in figure 6.4, we position a second clock GC2, synchronized with GC1, a distance of 0.95 light seconds to the right of GC1, in the direction of travel of the spaceship. (0.95 light seconds = $2.85\text{x}10^5$ kilometers, about

> 45 earth radii.) The time I measure on GC2 when your spaceship passes it is the distance between CG1 and GC2 divided by the velocity of the spaceship. Then, 0.95 light seconds divided by a velocity of 0.95c is 1 second or equivalently 2.85 x 10^5 km/0.95c = 1 second. Use the time dilation formula to find the time on your clock SC. In the time dilation formula, the one second in my frame corresponds to t and we need to find t_0, the time you measure in your frame. With v = 0.95c, we find t_0 = 0.31 seconds. My clock reads 1 second while yours only reads 0.31 seconds. Your clock runs slower than mine! Although I will not make the effort here, this slowing of clocks is completely symmetric. When you on the spaceship look at my clocks on the ground, they run slower for you, as it must be when there are no preferred frames.

It does not matter whether we use clocks based on light, atomic physics, nuclear physics, Newtonian mechanics, or biological processes: *moving clocks are measured to run slower than stationary clocks.*

Although it took more than thirty years after Einstein's 1905 paper for direct experimental confirmation of these results, special relativity has been confirmed with extraordinary accuracy in a wide variety of experiments. In fact, the Global Positioning System (GPS) must correct for the time dilation of the clocks in its satellites and thus offers a continuous confirmation of the theory. So when you successfully use the GPS in your car, on your boat, or on your camping trip, you are confirming the time-dilation formula.

The question that naturally comes to mind is, "Which is the more fundamental or more real time interval, t (time as measured by an observer that sees the clocking moving with velocity v) or t_0 (time as measured by an observer at rest with respect to the clock)?" Or, stated in another way, "Is not t_0 more real or truer than t?" Relativity is both unequivocal and emphatic in stating that *no time interval is more real or truer than any other.* There is no time interval more "intrinsic" to the clock than any other. They all have equal validity or reality, and there is nothing special about t_0, the time as measured by an observer at rest with respect to the clock. Time intervals only have meaning as they are measured by a particular observer in a given reference frame, and they vary according to

FIGURE 6.5.
Albert Einstein, the father of relativity (Courtesy AIP Emilio Segre Visual Archives)

the frame. We have to give up the idea of a time that is intrinsic to a given clock. In Middle Way language, we would say that time intervals do not have any intrinsic value or that they do not interdependently exist. They depend radically upon the reference frame from which they are observed and only have meaning in that frame.

Einstein's 1905 paper on special relativity was so revolutionary that it was greeted by many with shock and disbelief. How could time, which was always considered to have an absolute or intrinsic reality, be only relationally defined? In fact, in the early 1930s, several prominent physicists and Nazi sympathizers, two of whom were Nobel Prize winners in physics, mounted a campaign to disparage relativity (both special and general) as "Jewish physics." How could they justify that, given the two axioms from which the entire theory of special relativity follows? How distorted even great minds can become when an evil ideology overtakes them!

Once we have the time dilation formula, it takes only a couple of steps to show that lengths, masses, and energies are also dependent upon the reference frame from which they are measured. We normally think that time, length, mass, and energy are the most fundamental attributes of a thing. In fact, all these properties are strongly dependent upon the reference frame from which they are measured. *They have no intrinsic value, no independent existence.* It is not that they have some intrinsic value and that different observers view that value from their own particular point of view. Because there is no preferred reference frame, no one value has any privilege over any other. In Middle Way language, we would say they are totally lacking in independent or inherent existence. They do not exist from their own side but only in relationship to a particular reference frame. The Middle Way and relativity could not be more compatible on this point.

I conclude with a brief discussion of the relativity of simultaneity, another important feature of special relativity. Two events are simultaneous when they occur at the same instant for a given observer. For example, two widely separated traffic lights turn red at the same time for me. It is easy to show that simultaneity is deeply dependent upon the reference frame from which the events are observed. This means that my pair of simultaneous events is not simultaneous for other moving observers. For example, for an observer moving relative to the traffic lights, one light will turn red before the other. This has all sorts of interesting implications. Let's look briefly at just one.

The present moment is defined by the collection of all the events happening at the same time. So, for me, the traffic lights turn red, friends in Europe board an airplane, and a mouse eats a seed in my yard. All these events (and much more) constitute the present moment for me. If you are a second observer moving with respect to me, because of the relativity of simultaneity, you would have a different set of events for the present moment. Not only are the properties of the events (such as their mass, length, time, and energy) frame dependent, so too are the collection of events that constitute the present moment. The present moment, both the individual events and the collection of those events, is also relative and therefore lacks independent existence. The conclusions of relativity and the Middle Way are both radical and in full agreement.

A well-known book is entitled *The Power of Now: A Guide to Spiritual Enlightenment.*[3] Knowledge of special relativity or the Middle Way will keep you from considering that "now" as independently or inherently existent.

A Puzzle about the Nature of Time

When I was a young boy, I was very fond of yo-yos. I could do all sorts of tricks with them and spent hours leaning new ones and perfecting old ones. I once stole a beautiful new golden Duncan yo-yo from a store. I certainly am ashamed now of that event, but it cannot be undone. Whatever learning, confessing, or reinterpreting is done, it cannot change the fact that I stole that yo-yo. Although I can still vividly see that yo-yo and feel remorse, there is no going back. Let's hope recalling it will help me in the future, where there is some chance that I can improve.

We all appreciate this qualitative difference between the past and the future. I started this chapter recalling that past events have a clear fixity about them. Each event seems as if it were glued to a ribbon that stretches back into the distant past, and it seems as though there were a metaphorical "arrow of time" pointing along the ribbon from the past, through the present, and into the indefinite future. How different space seems with its uniform properties in all directions.

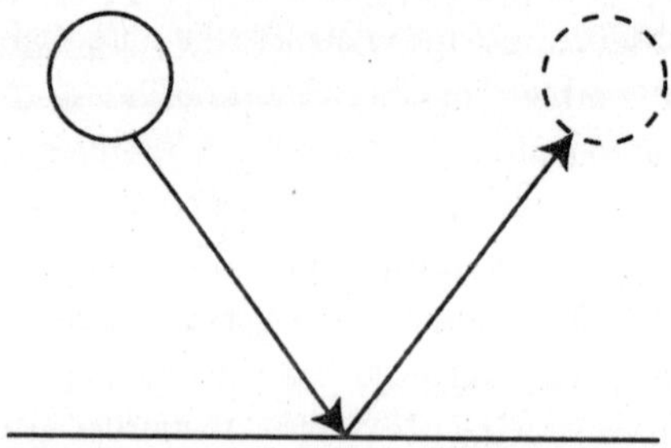

FIGURE 6.6. *Bouncing ball*

All this appears natural and obvious. The puzzle comes when we look at the nature of time in physics. Let's take the simple experiment of bouncing a ball off the floor at an angle as shown in figure 6.6. Let the ball be thrown from the left (the solid sphere), bounce off the floor at an angle and end up on the right (the dashed sphere). Choose a lively Super Ball that loses almost no energy in the actual collision. If a movie of this little experiment is run backwards, then the ball would start on the right and end up on the left. This time-reversed motion obeys all the laws of physics, and nothing seems strange about it. In fact, if you did not know the movie was running backwards, you would have no way to tell it was reversed motion from just looking at the ball.

Now take a more complex example. Our sun revolves around the center of our galaxy in an approximately circular orbit. It takes about 250 million years to complete one full orbit. At the same time, the planets revolve around the sun with each planet simultaneously rotating on its own axis. Imagine a movie of this complex motion being run backwards. Everything would be reversed: the planets rotating around each axis, the planets revolving around the sun, and the sun's orbiting around the center of the galaxy. However, all these time-reversed motions would obey all the laws of Newtonian mechanics and nothing in the backward running movie would seem strange. All this can be summarized by saying that the laws of mechanics are time-reversible. For this reason, whether bouncing a ball or considering the solar system's motion, the time evolution of the system can run either forward or backward and still obey all the appropriate laws of physics.

For a quantum mechanical system, consider the interferometer I used in discussing causality in the previous chapter. All the photons moving through the interferometer could be run in the reverse direction without violating any laws of physics. All this is possible because the laws of quantum mechanics are also time-reversible, as are all the laws in physics.[4]

But there is a paradox here. Consider an egg sitting on a tilted table. Soon, the egg rolls off the edge and splatters on the floor. If we film this breaking of an egg and run that backward, it will look very strange. Nobody sees eggs spread out on the floor suddenly reassemble themselves and hop up on a table. Breaking an egg is certainly not time-reversible or time-symmetric. Nor have we ever seen rotten fruit gradually return to its fresh state, nor old bodies nor rotten teeth become whole again. So, our puzzle is that the fundamental underlying laws of physics are time-reversible, but we clearly experience time-irreversible events, whether the breaking of an egg or the breaking of our moral standards.

Time Asymmetry out of Symmetric Interactions

Rotting, whether of vegetables, teeth, or our entire bodies, is an irreversible process. Since the quantum mechanical laws governing the chemical changes of rotting are time-symmetric, this is mysterious. The great

Austrian physicist Ludwig Boltzmann made the first significant progress in understanding this mystery. He realized that irreversibility comes from reversible underlying laws only when you have large numbers of particles in the system.

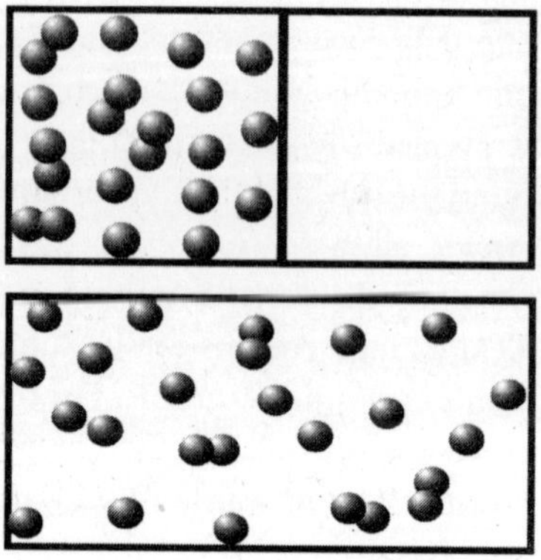

FIGURE 6.7. *Isolated boxes*

Boltzmann started by considering a simple box containing many gas particles governed by Newton's laws. In analyzing this system, he assumed that it was totally isolated from the rest of the universe. There were no influences of the universe on the box and its contents or vice versa. In other words, the box was energetically isolated from the rest of the universe so that no energy moved from the universe to the box or vice versa. Remember that the idea of a fully isolated system is offensive to any Middle Way Buddhist, who always stresses that objects are defined by their relationships and dependencies. As we will see, this isolation cannot be upheld in physics and dramatic conclusions follow from this. For now, let us follow Boltzmann when he imagines a partition in the middle of the box with all the particles in just one half of the box (as shown in the top of figure 6.7). The other half is totally empty.

To proceed further we need to understand the concept of entropy or measure of disorder. The more disorder, the less knowledge we have about the details of the system, the higher the entropy. Take my desk as an example. When I am working hard, papers, books, journals, writing tools, computer disks, and so forth pile up and increase the general disorder or entropy of my desk. When I can't stand the disordered or high-entropy state any longer, in large part because it is so difficult to find anything, I spend time and energy setting it in order and thereby decreasing its entropy. As we all know, decreasing entropy requires the expenditure of energy.

Upon removing the partition separating the gas particles in Boltzmann's box, the overwhelmingly most probable configurations of the new equilibrium condition involve the gas distributed evenly throughout the box. This is a condition of higher entropy because we have less precise information about the location of the particles. In principle, it is possible, although exceedingly unlikely, for the gas to bunch up in only one corner of the box. However, it is overwhelmingly more probable that it will attain a new equilibrium configuration diffused evenly throughout the box (as shown in the bottom of figure 6.7). Such equilibrium states have maximum entropy. This is an example of how *a disturbed system moves toward a new equilibrium with higher entropy.*

Consider a more familiar example. Imagine a completely ordered deck of cards with all the cards of a particular suit together and arranged starting with two, three, four, on up to the jack, queen, king, and ace. This completely ordered deck is in a state of very low entropy. Now imagine continuously shuffling the cards for a full ten minutes. At the end of that time, it is overwhelmingly likely that the cards will be in a state of much greater disorder or entropy. That is the normal reason for shuffling the cards in the first place. Although it is possible that, after ten minutes of shuffling, the cards could end up completely ordered again, this is exceedingly unlikely. Here again, we see that disturbed systems naturally evolve to states of high probability corresponding to increased entropy.

Through this line of reasoning, Boltzmann proved the famous second law of thermodynamics, which says that any isolated system's entropy must either stay the same or increase. Therefore, after removing the partition, the gas is overwhelmingly likely to go to a state of greater entropy. This increase in entropy defines the direction of the arrow of time. *Time advances in the same direction in which entropy increases—what we call the future.* This does not deny that there are local decreases in entropy, like the growth of a child, but the global entropy relentlessly increases with time.

For several years, I taught Colgate University's junior-senior level course on statistical physics. We used the standard textbook and followed Boltzmann's derivation of the second law of thermodynamics, with the appropriate level of mathematical sophistication. Recently, I found that there have been arguments dating as far back as 1877 that showed Boltzmann's derivation has serious problems. I review some of these issues elsewhere in nontechnical language.[5] Here, I take a different approach and follow an elegant and simple argument by P. C. W. Davies,[6] which can be skipped without undue loss of continuity. As we will shortly see, entropy increases, but not the way Boltzmann thought. Why several revisions of this famous statistical physics text persist in this error is a mystery.

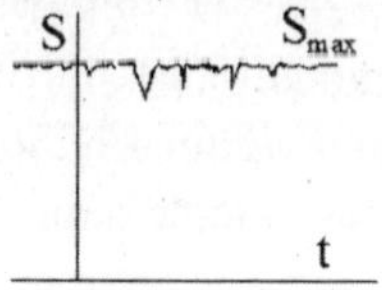

FIGURE 6.8

The basic difficulty, which can be seen in several independent ways, is that completely isolated systems, like the box of gas, can generate no directionality with respect to time because of the time-symmetric laws governing the system. Figure 6.8 displays the equilibrium entropy S, of an isolated box of gas plotted versus time t. It shows that the random gas motions give occasional deviations below the maximum entropy S_{max}. Although unlikely, the random motions spontaneously generate states of greater order or lower entropy, which are then brought back to maximum disorder by the same randomization. This is like the shuffling of playing cards that, on very rare occasions, puts them into states of greater order, with continued shuffling returning them to disorder.

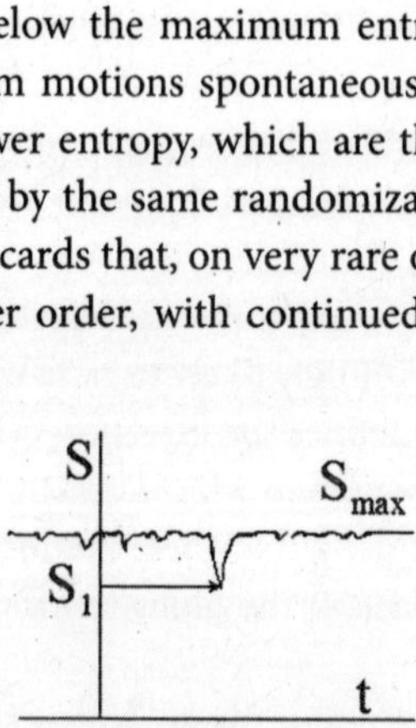

FIGURE 6.9

Now imagine the following experiment illustrated in figure 6.9. We patiently monitor the system until its entropy spontaneously drops to the value S_1 or below at a time t_1. Since we choose S_1 low enough, this could take a long time. The virtue of choosing a small value of S_1 is that, once it occurs, we know we are very likely to be near the bottom of a dip in the entropy curve, rather than part-way down a larger dip. This is simply because even larger dips are so much less likely. At t_1, when the low entropy S_1 occurs, since we are very likely at the minimum of a dip, entropy increases either before or after t_1. More explicitly, at time $t_1 + \varepsilon$, where ε is some small time interval, the entropy increases. From the point of view of t_1, the time $t_1 + \varepsilon$ is in the future, since that is the time where entropy is increasing. However, the entropy was also greater at $t_1 - \varepsilon$, so this time could also be considered the future since time advances in the direction of increasing entropy. Now what happened to the arrow of time? It certainly cannot point in both directions at once. Here we see that the symmetry of the underlying laws of physics gives no directionality to entropy increase or time. In this way, we can see that the great Boltzmann's analysis is fatally flawed. An equilibrium system isolated from the rest of the universe cannot distinguish the future from the past.

As Thomas Gold, one of my professors from graduate school at Cornell University, showed many years ago, the main problem with Boltzman's derivation lies in assuming we can have a totally isolated system independent of interaction with the universe. Gold showed that we must always account for interactions between thermodynamic systems and the universe. For example, how did Boltzmann's box get into the low-entropy state of all particles in just one half (top of figure 6.7)? This did not result from just waiting a long time for random motions to throw the gas all to one side, but from Boltzmann evacuating one half and placing gas in the other. Preparing the box in a low-entropy state requires energy and generates more entropy elsewhere in the universe. For example, Boltzmann consumed calories from lunch and radiated energy from himself and his equipment that eventually went into deep space. In other words, the box had its entropy put into a low condition by processes outside itself but at the expense of energy and a greater entropy increase elsewhere in the universe.

Let me give an example closer to the garden. I walk in the garden to check on whether rabbits have eaten the carrots. My footprint in the soft soil gives it more order and structure, thus lowering its entropy. However, this lower entropy comes from a much greater generation of entropy from my metabolic processes that expend energy and eventually degrade to heat radiated to the universe.

Physicists now realize that the energy emitted into deep space from our activities is only possible in an expanding universe. To appreciate this, consider being in a large forest on level ground. Although there is plenty of space between the trees, when we look deeply into the forest, our line of sight will eventually fall on a tree trunk. In every direction, at eye level, we see brown tree trunks. In contrast, imagine that each tree can pick up its roots and move away from the other trees. In such a forest in which the distance between every tree was constantly increasing with time, not every line of sight would fall on a tree trunk.

Analogously, in a static or nonexpanding universe, any line of sight away from the earth, when extended far enough, would land on a star surface. In this case, rather than seeing tree trunks in every direction, we would see stars filling all space. Since light also travels toward the earth on the same lines of sight, the effective temperature of deep space would be that of the surface of stars, which is typically 6,000K, rather than the 3K it actually has. In fact, because the universe is actually expanding, we see plenty of cool, dark sky.

Since entropy can only increase when energy moves from high- to low-temperature regions, the simple process of radiating our body's energy into space would be blocked in a static or nonexpanding universe. In other words, if the sphere of the sky as seen from earth is a higher temperature than the earth, there is no way to radiate our waste heat away. Then there would be neither a Boltzmann nor the ability to reduce entropy locally in the box by generating more entropy elsewhere in the universe. All systems organizing themselves or decreasing their entropy, whether the growing of a carrot, a snowflake, or a child, are decreasing entropy in one location that must be accompanied by a greater entropy generation in another. All this would be blocked in a static universe. Therefore, the first point is to appreciate that the expansion of the universe is essential for entropy to increase and time to have an arrow.

What causes the sun and other stars to be in a low-entropy condition in the first place? This occurs because, in the first three minutes of the big bang, the expansion rate of the universe was faster than the nuclear-generation rates. Then, when nearly all the helium (about 25% of the total mass of the universe) was formed, the universe expanded so quickly that, after three minutes, it was too cool for nuclear reactions to occur. If the expansion and associated cooling were much slower, then all the matter in the universe would have been processed into iron-56, a very stable isotope of iron, an inert and high-entropy condition with no differentiation into different elements. Then the stars would not shine, there would be no great entropy gradients in the universe, no time asymmetry, and, of course, no life as we know it. Therefore, for entropy to increase in the normal way and for time to have an arrow, two conditions are necessary. First, the universe must be expanding on the largest possible scales. Second, the cosmic expansion had to happen faster than the nuclear reaction rates for there to be low-entropy stars. *Therefore, local time asymmetry, such as the decay of any biological system, from carrots to our own bodies, must be accounted for by connecting it to the overall expansion of the universe and its very earliest evolution.*

This extraordinary beautiful result has many technical twists and turns. However, the central idea is clear: increasing entropy and time asymmetry owe their existence to the very largest and earliest processes in the universe, to its continued expansion and its rapid early expansion. This is a long way from the notion of an isolated and noninteracting system, initially assumed by Boltzmann. In this way, when you put cold milk into your coffee and the mixture comes to the same temperature and to a higher entropy than when the fluids were separated, you are profiting from the universe's ongoing expansion and its earliest cooling before iron-56 could form. Similarly, that we must all face the irreversible process of death, with its massive entropy increase, is traceable to the largest scale expansion and the earliest processes in the universe. In other words, the impermanence and decay found all around us is due to the most distant and earliest process in the universe. This level of scientific interconnectedness and dependency could not be imagined by Tsongkhapa and the early founders of the Middle Way, yet it would surely make them smile.

As I have stressed, emptiness, the complete lack of independent existence, by its very nature guarantees continuous change. The impermanence directly expressing emptiness is a law of the universe. However, by itself, change does not tell us why there is an arrow of time. Why do we inevitably succumb to old age, sickness, and death, as the Buddhists so frequently remind us? In principle, with emptiness, we could get younger and healthier, for that too is change. However, because the universe is expanding, the big bang happened quickly, and we are intimately connected to the universe, there is an arrow of time. Of course, the great Buddhist teachers did not need to understand the arrow of time to proclaim the truth of old age, sickness, and death. They just looked around. Nevertheless, it helps strengthen my appreciation of emptiness to think that something so intimate and personal as my inevitable decline is connected to the largest and earliest process in the universe. In chapter 4, I quoted Desmond Tutu as saying "We are made for a delicate network of interdependence." Now we must appreciate that this "delicate network" stretches to the farthest reaches of the universe and back to the earliest moments of the big bang.

It is important to appreciate that irreversible processes are also essential to life. If metabolic processes did not irreversibly transform my lunch, not only would I get indigestion, I could not live. There are innumerable other irreversible biological process from the growth and repair of cells to the secretion of hormones. This echoes the pivotal idea in the Middle Way that says it is the very emptiness of independent existence, the very interdependent nature of phenomena at the most fundamental level, which allows them to function. That emptiness at the heart of all sustains me as a biological entity and also destroys me. More generally, the people making this book, along with the reader, are possible because of the irreversible processes that give time its arrow. Indeed, as Borges says, time "is a fire that consumes me, but I am the fire."

7. Toward the Union of Love and Knowledge

Introduction

Every morning I meditate, make breakfast, and then read the electronic edition of *The New York Times*. Is the value of meditation erased by my immersion in the misery and cruelty of the news? I do sometimes doubt the sanity of my routine. However, I tell myself that part of my job as a professor, especially one deeply involved in Colgate's General Education Program, demands knowledge of current affairs. I also take some solace in knowing that His Holiness the Dalai Lama listens to several sources of news on his short-wave radio while eating breakfast, even when he travels.[1] On the other hand, that His Holiness can immerse himself in the news and not get overwhelmed by the wretchedness and brutality of it all hardly means the same is possible for me.

In this final chapter, I review and deepen our discussion of the relationship between modern physics and the Middle Way. I conclude by discussing how this expedition through the heart of modern physics and Tibetan Buddhism—from quantum mechanics, relativity, and cosmology to emptiness, disintegratedness, and compassion—might apply to today's painfully polarized world and how we might move toward a union of love and knowledge.

To deepen the connections between the Middle Way and physics, I turn to the famous delayed-choice experiments of John A. Wheeler, surely one of the simplest and most dramatic experiments to probe the foundations of quantum mechanics.[2] As we will see, understanding these experiments drives us into the heart of quantum mechanics and simultaneously into the arms of the Middle Way.

A Delayed-Choice Experiment

Let us start from the beginning with a beam splitter, which I discussed in chapter 5 in the material with a gray background. (If you already understand the function of a beam splitter then I can only take comfort in a saying of the great Italian-American physicist Enrico Fermi who said, "Never underestimate the pleasure people get from hearing something they already know.") This device allows half of the intensity of the incoming beam of light through and reflects the other half, as shown in figure 7.1 below. In other words, if one hundred photons per second are moving from left to right as they enter the beam splitter then, on the average, fifty per second are transmitted to the right and fifty per second are reflected down. Of course, because of the randomness at the heart of quantum mechanics, we cannot predict which photons are transmitted and which are reflected. Nevertheless, on average, they are equally likely to be transmitted as reflected.

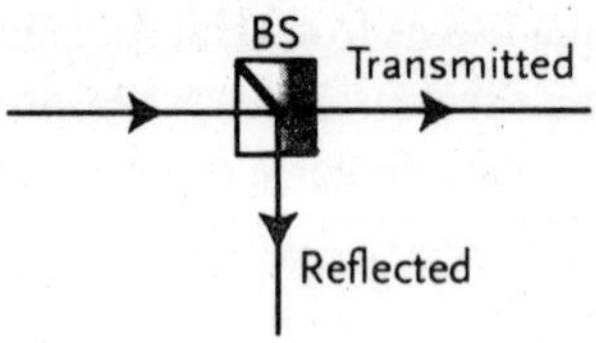

Figure 7.1. ***Beam splitter***

With one beam splitter and two fully reflecting mirrors, we can make the interferometer shown in figure 7.2. Then, light comes in from the left, and the first beam splitter transmits half of the light to the right and reflects half downward. Follow the reflected light moving downward. This beam strikes a fixed, fully reflecting mirror set at a 45-degree angle with respect to the incoming beam. Such a mirror reflects the entire light incident on it and turns the beam from going straight down to going directly to the right and into detector 1. Next, from the beam splitter, follow the light moving to the right. It reflects off a fully reflecting mirror also set at 45 degrees with respect to the incoming beam. This mirror, however, is moveable. Nevertheless, it reflects the beam directly downward into detector 2.

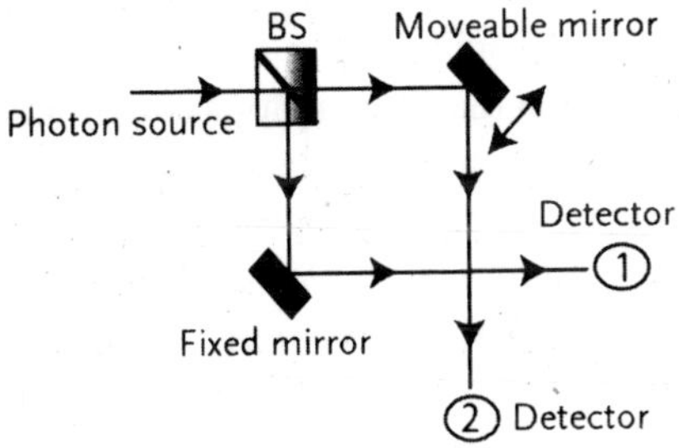

FIGURE 7.2. *Interferometer*

With this interferometer, if you had one hundred photons per second in the input beam, on average, half (fifty photons/second) would be registered in detector 1 and half in detector 2. What is critical for our purposes is that we know that any photons captured in detector 1 must have come through the interferometer by the left path—the light reflected off the beam splitter downward and then rightward off the fully reflective fixed mirror. By the same reasoning, any photons registered in detector 2 must have followed the right path—the light transmitted from the beam splitter to the fully reflective moveable mirror and then downward. So monitoring the signals in detectors 1 and 2 gives complete information on which path the light took in getting to the detector. The light is displaying its particle nature by going via the left path or the right path but never both.

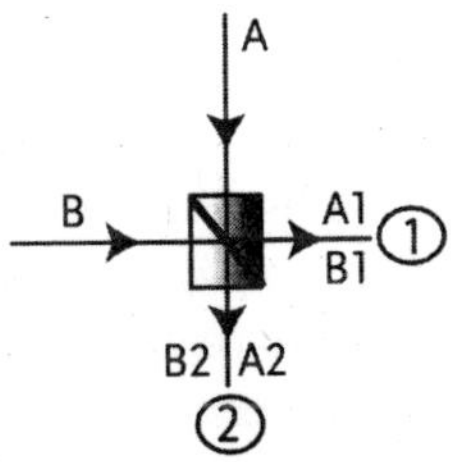

FIGURE 7.3. *Intersection beam splitter*

Next, take another beam splitter and place it in the intersection of the two beams, just before they go into the detectors. Figure 7.3 shows what occurs in that second beam splitter. Label beam B the light from the lower fully reflecting fixed mirror. Half of beam B is transmitted into B1 going into detector 1, while the other half reflects downward into B2 going into detector 2. Label beam A the light moving downward off the fully reflecting moveable mirror. Half of this beam reflects into A1 going into detector 1, while the other half transmits into A2 going into detector 2.

With two beam splitters in place, what does a signal in detector 1 tell about which path the photon took? It tells us nothing since either path could give a signal at detector 1. It is important to appreciate that the left path, beam B, transmits B1 into detector 1, while the right path, beam A, reflects A1 into detector 1. Of course, both paths also contribute to registrations in detector 2 (beams A2 and B2). Therefore, the interferometer with the bottom beam splitter in place gives no path information.

Now, just consider detector 1. If we adjust the moveable, fully reflective mirror so that the left and right path lengths are the same, then the beams A1 and B1 are in phase, and they gave a signal of maximum strength at detector 1. (Signal "strength" means photon counts per second.) Recall that, with waves in phase, when their crests and troughs arrive at the same time at a given location, the resulting waves constructively interfere, giving maximum amplitude. In contrast, when the right and left path lengths differ by a half a wavelength, then A1 and B1 are out of phase and destructively interfere at detector 1, giving no signal. Intermediate differences between the left and right paths give signals between maximum strength and zero. Plotting the signal strength at detector 1 versus the path length difference between the left and right paths gives beautiful sinusoidal curves like that in figure 5.7 from chapter 5. This clearly shows that, when we do not know path information, light displays its wave nature through interference phenomena.

Okay, so our interferometer gives path information with the second beam splitter left out, while putting in the second beam splitter gives interference phenomena. By leaving out or putting in the second beam splitter, we can choose to display the particle or wave nature of light but never both at the same time. Here is the familiar display of complementary properties of quantum objects depending upon our choice of experiment.

Now comes the delayed-choice part of the experiment. Wheeler asks what happens when we decide at the very last femtosecond whether to put the second beam splitter into the interferometer or leave it out. (A femtosecond is 10^{-15} seconds.) Our last femtosecond decision determines whether we view the particle or wave nature of light. By waiting until just before the light gets to the detector, we can be sure that the light has already been reflected from the fully reflective mirrors. Wait! Does our last-moment decision affect the behavior of light in the past? Is there some backward causality here where present actions (putting in the second beam splitter or not) affect the previous behavior of light? (Please make sure you see that there is a delightful puzzle here!) Before answering this provocative question, let me follow Wheeler and dramatize the situation by putting it into a cosmological context.

A Cosmological Delayed-choice Experiment

In his general relativity, Einstein found that massive bodies bend light. The first experimental test of general relativity came in 1919, when Sir Arthur Eddington measured the bending of starlight around our sun during a total eclipse. (You need an eclipse so that the sun's light does not overwhelm the background stars.) When Eddington found the bending predicted by general relativity, Einstein became an international celebrity.

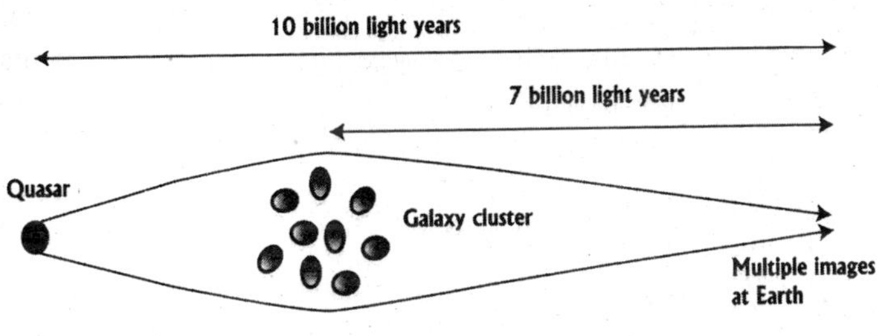

FIGURE 7.4. *Galaxy cluster as gravitational lens*

Even more dramatic examples of light bending occur in cosmology, where clusters of galaxies act as a gravitational lens to focus light from very distant quasars. Quasars are extremely bright and compact objects powered by giant black holes at their core. Figure 7.4 shows the geometry for a gravitational lens. In this example, the quasar is 10 billion light years from earth, while the galaxy cluster is 7 billion light years away. (To put this into context, our solar system formed about 4.5 billion years ago, long after the light from that quasar started on its way to us.) When the intervening mass (here, a galaxy cluster) is not spherically symmetric and not perfectly aligned with the light source (quasar), the bending gives multiple images of the distant quasar. Notice how the gravitational bending acts like an interferometer for the quasar light. Rather than beam splitters and mirrors, the galaxy cluster focuses light into multiple images at earth.

Although there are many examples of gravitational lensing, the best example was announced in the spring of 2006, when the Hubble Space Telescope found multiple images of a quasar gravitationally lensed by the galaxy cluster SDSS J1004+4112.[3] The picture in figure 7.5 extends about 1/60 of the moon's diameter and shows five images of one quasar found with Hubble—the four white, bright circular images and the redder one in the center. I have placed large white arrows pointing to two of the quasar images. Analysis of the system reveals that these two images come from light bending around opposite sides of the galaxy cluster, just as shown in figure 7.4.

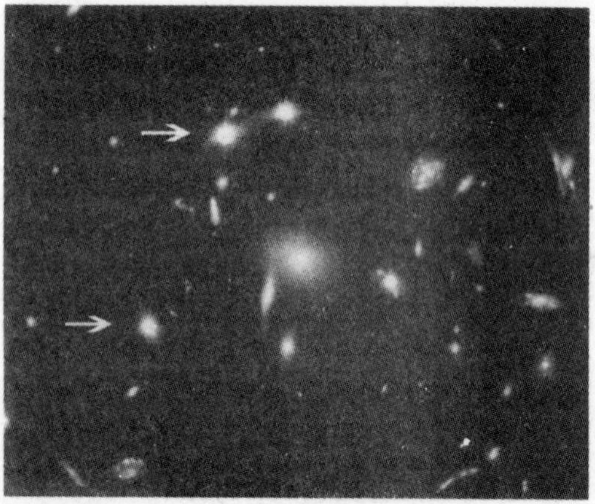

FIGURE 7.5.
Quasar multiple images

Imagine an experiment in which we focus two separate telescopes (with their own detectors) on the two quasar images with white arrows pointing at them. In such a case, the situation is just like having two detectors in the interferometer of figure 7.2. We can tell around which side of the galaxy cluster the photons went. We are observing path information or the particle nature of the light. As mentioned above with respect to the geometry in this example, those photons left the galaxy cluster's vicinity about 7 billion years ago, long before even the formation of our solar system.

Now imagine a different experiment in which we optically direct the two quasar images into a beam splitter to get interference effects. In this case, we cannot see two distinct images corresponding to the two paths, but our signal strength depends upon the path length differences for going around one side of the galaxy cluster in comparison to going around the other side. In other words, in the first experiment with two detectors, we find out which path the photon took (particle properties of the light) and in the second experiment, we are get interference effects (wave properties of the light).

Does this mean that, if I decide today to use two detectors and get particle information and then tomorrow to use a beam splitter and get wave information, I am affecting the photon's behavior when it was in the vicinity of the gravitational lens some 7 billion years ago? In other words, does what I do today affect what occurred more than 2 billion years before the earth was formed?

Surely, this is too bizarre for even quantum mechanics! What is going on here? The answer is that we have illegitimately projected an independent existence onto the photon. We made the false mental picture of light with intrinsic properties (such as a wave or a particle) as it was passing the galaxy cluster independent of our experimental arrangement. I also confess to using misleading language, such as "the photon left the galaxy cluster's vicinity about 7 billion years ago" and other similar statements. Ordinary language is usually built from statements that unconsciously assume independently existing objects. However, the delayed-choice experiment, within the cosmological context, makes it clear that we cannot attribute definite properties to quantum objects independently of the entire observational situation. Quantum objects do not independently or inherently exist, or "exist from their own side," as they say in the Middle Way. They are only defined within the context of an actual measurement, within a relationship to a specific experimental arrangement. Just as in chapter 4, where we were examining quantum nonlocality, we see here in the delayed-choice experiments that nature refuses our false projection of inherent existence. Wheeler quotes Bohr in summarizing the situation:

> In today's words Bohr's point—and the central point of quantum theory—can be put into a single, simple sentence. "No elementary phenomenon is a phenomenon until it is registered (observed) phenomenon." It is wrong to speak of the "route" of the photon in the experiment with the beam splitter. It is wrong to attribute tangibility to the photon in all its travel from the point of entry to its last instant of flight. A phenomenon is not yet a phenomenon until it has been brought to a close by an irreversible act of amplification, such as the blackening of a grain of silver bromide emulsion or the triggering of a photodetector. In broader terms, we find that nature at the quantum level is not a machine that goes its inexorable way. Instead, what answer we get depends on the question we put, the experiment we arrange, the registering device we choose. We are inescapably involved in bringing about that which appears to be happening.[4]

Or as Wheeler says a few pages later:

> It is wrong to think of that past as "already existing" in all detail. The past has no existence except as it is recorded in the present. By deciding what questions our quantum registering equipment shall put in the present, we have an undeniable choice in what we have the right to say about the past.[5]

Here we go again! The mind has the inveterate tendency to conceive of light as "'already existing' in all detail," to consider light as inherently existing. Yet, quantum mechanics, the most fundamental theory in all of science, forces us to renounce that view, that false projection. Instead, we must understand quantum objects as dependently related, as in part determined by the questions we ask and the interaction we choose with nature. Recall that emptiness is a nonaffirming negation. There is no replacement of phenomena by some higher reality, only the appreciation that all things, without exception, are empty and dependently interrelated. In the same way, quantum mechanics does not give a detailed picture underlying the phenomena. Such models would only be inappropriate reifications or objectifications, attempts at building mechanical models from independently existing elements. Instead, we must be content with appreciating the radical interconnectedness of all phenomena and not seek any deeper reality that inherently exists. Part of this radical interconnectedness of nature is, as the delayed-choice experiments show, connection to the observer and the questions she asks.

In thinking about this experiment, we must be careful not to fall into the trap of admitting the dependent and relational nature of light, while unconsciously attributing intrinsic characteristics such as mass and shape to the galaxy cluster. Recall from our brief excursion into special relativity that mass, length, and time intervals do not have intrinsic or objective values independent of an observer's reference frame. Not only is the nature of light deeply dependent upon the question we pose through our experimental arrangement, but the properties of the galaxy cluster are also defined only within the observer's reference frame. The galaxies neither individually nor in a cluster have any reference-frame-independent values for their size, mass, and time intervals.

It is very difficult to break our inveterate habit of projecting inherent existence or of believing in definite properties independent of our experiment. Despite these habitual tendencies, modern physics demands a radical revision of our worldview, one extraordinarily close to the Middle Way doctrine of emptiness.

As we have seen in several chapters of this book, projecting inherent or independent existence is scientific error. With enough effort, nature corrects us and leads us to an interconnected, interdependent, or empty view of the universe. More generally, in the Middle Way, error always leads to suffering. As discussed toward the end of chapter 3, a realization of the error of projecting independent existence and how it causes suffering, for both ourself and others, naturally leads to universal compassion, to a firm commitment to relieve the suffering of all sentient beings. Here we see how a deep knowledge of nature generates universal compassion. In this way, we move toward the union of love and knowledge, the subject of our final section.

Toward the Union of Love and Knowledge

It is 1990, and my wife and I are buying vegetables in a market in Kanchipuram, India. Color and motion are everywhere. Women in vibrant saris display their produce on the ground, as in the photograph shown below. People wrangling over prices, good-natured shouting, and children running everywhere. My wife puts her newly purchased beans (see the lower left of the photograph) into a Ziploc plastic bag. The woman selling the beans is obviously impressed with those plastic bags with the zipper-locking seal. We show her how they work. She clearly would like one of those bags. We give her a big zipper-locking bag, and she breaks out into the loveliest smile, thanks us profusely, and I take her photograph.

FIGURE 7.6.
A lover of technology

Whether in the developing world or the modern, industrialized world, everybody desires technology and its promise of greater happiness. Whether it is a youth desiring the latest digital music player, the poor Indian woman desiring a plastic Ziplock bag, or the AIDS sufferer desiring modern medicine, the allure of technology is irresistible. We may not always make the wisest choices, but there is no doubt that we all desire technology and its promise of a better life.

Furthermore, when a nation seeks prosperity and prestige, it invariably wants the science that underlies the technology, the theory beneath the applications. For example, the first step is typically the desire for modern electronics, whether a music player or a computer. The next step is mastering the quantum mechanics, the science underlying the electronic applications. Even the most traditional societies, whether north or south, east or west, want a skilled cadre of scientists and their supporting facilities. As I pointed out in chapter 1, science is built upon principles and experiments that transcend national boundaries, religious, and personal preferences; therefore, portability is at its very heart. (This is not to say that science does not have its own presuppositions.) Thus, desire and portability guarantee that science and technology spread rapidly and relentlessly throughout the globe.

Unfortunately, scientific knowledge is often disconnected from its most humane application, the relief of suffering. Our planet has the knowledge and resources to solve most of the evils of poverty, a few of which I sketched in chapter 2. Nevertheless, we allow enormous inequalities to exist and permit widespread suffering that our knowledge could easily alleviate. To use Peter Singer's image, the human race is like a man ignoring a drowning little girl rather than making the small sacrifice needed to save her life. Simply put, our knowledge is disconnected from love, from a genuine concern for others, from simple kindness.

My daily reading of *The New York Times* reveals more than the neglect and indifference of our species toward the less fortunate. The headlines tell of far too many instances of the most evil savagery and destruction of each other and our planet. Despite the many unrecorded acts of kindness, both large and small, we can have no illusions about the brutality that flourishes in today's world. In chapter 4, I quoted the internationally famous physicist, the late David Bohm, who wrote: ". . . the widespread and pervasive distinctions between people . . . now preventing mankind from working together for the common good, and indeed, even for survival, have . . . their origin in a kind of thought that treats things as inherently divided, disconnected, and 'broken up' into yet smaller constituent parts. Each part is considered to be essentially independent and self-existent."[6] In Middle Way language, he is claiming that our belief in independent or inherent existence is threatening our very survival. Bohm is referring to the worldview of classical or Newtonian physics that reinforces our innate tendency to project inherent existence into everything from photons to our own personality.

In contrast, quantum mechanics and relativity tell us that, rather than each element being "essential independent or self-existent," all phenomena are interdependent, defined primarily by their relationship to other elements of the world and our observation. Whether you are considering photons or the length of your arm, things do not have any independent or inherent existence. In Middle Way language, they lack or are empty of inherent existence and are defined by their relationships and our mental designation. Despite the significant differences between science and Buddhism discussed in chapter 1 and the divergence between the Middle Way and quantum mechanical views on causality discussed in chapter 5, quantum mechanics and relativity are in thoroughgoing agreement with Middle Way emptiness on this point—not just in broad outline but in terms of the most fundamental principles. Just as the belief in independent existence leads to suffering, this new scientific worldview, which is inevitably spreading throughout the world, must also have consequences. In the Middle Way, there is an intimate, unbreakable bond between the wisdom of emptiness and its expression in universal compassion. Practitioners of that teaching hold that all philosophic principles must have moral consequences, and, thus, the truth of emptiness must be expressed in compassionate action.

Unfortunately, the average person in the street has little interest in the implications of quantum mechanics and relativity. What is more, revolutions in our worldview take a long time to reach all parts of the population. Both these truths forcefully struck me about two years ago while watching the sun sink into the Gulf of Mexico from a beach in western Florida with my dear uncle. He fought bravely in World War II, became a first-rate machinist, raised a family, and recently died. With some embarrassment, he asked me to explain the sunset. He did not understand how the earth rotates on its axis and revolves around the sun. It was clear that other members of my family on the beach that evening had the same question but were afraid to ask it. In a few minutes, I explained the sunset, but it was clearly unfamiliar territory. If several members of my family had not experienced the four-century-old Copernican revolution, how can we expect widespread appreciation of the current quantum revolution, which is both more difficult to understand and of greater consequence? Explaining the profound interconnectedness so vividly displayed in modern physics would have taken me a lot longer, and my chances of success would have been much smaller.

However, the importance of a scientific revolution cannot be determined by how widely it is understood or how difficult it is to explain. I suggest a Buddhist-inspired criterion for the importance of a scientific revolution and its associated worldview: the importance of a scientific revolution is its potential to reduce suffering in our daily lives. Although professors and their kind make a big point about how the Copernican revolution relativized our place in the universe and so forth, it has little or no practical consequences for the average person. Yes, in terms of an understanding of who we are and our place in the universe, the Copernican revolution is a major transformation, but it does not significantly reduce suffering. My uncle got along fine for more than eighty-five years without any idea of the Copernican revolution. My explaining it to him changed little in his life.

In contrast, consider the much younger germ theory of disease, which is little more than a century old. This theory tells us that microbes are the source of most diseases, rather than their being spontaneously generated or expressing God's wrath. This most important contribution of microbiology to modern health and to the relief of suffering has many practical consequences, even for those who understand nothing of microbiology. My uncle need not understand anything about microorganisms, but he does need to know how to keep wounds clean on the battlefield of the South Pacific or in his machine shop back home. In a similar way, he need not understand the complexities of quantum nonlocality or delayed-choice experiments, but he can understand the demand for kindness implied by the interdependence or emptiness of all phenomena. The germ theory of disease has significantly relieved suffering and, by my criterion, is a greater scientific revolution than that of Copernicus. But what has greater potential to relieve suffering than *nying je chenmo*, great compassion, the fruit of emptiness?

I am not discounting the latest "hardware applications" of modern physics. We are clear about their allure and their potential for both great help and harm. Rather, I am emphasizing the "software application," that the view of nature as profoundly interconnected and interdependent could promote a very different world than that described by David Bohm—one in which compassion more fully flowers. Of course, a scientific worldview is not on its own going to bring about an ideal world, but it can encourage us to move into a culture where kindness plays a bigger role. Thus, using the criterion of its potential to reduce suffering, any scientific revolution that establishes emptiness (as quantum mechanics and relativity do) is an important revolution.

My uncle had the ghastly job of killing Japanese soldiers in their bunkers with flamethrowers and grenades, but he was one of the kindest men I ever knew. It would take nothing to explain to him the idea that our noblest aspiration is to seek the welfare of all sentient beings. In fact, especially after much suffering toward the end of his life, he naturally understood and practiced kindness to all. I am thus suggesting that, in most cases, it is more important to emphasize the practical application of the scientific revolution than its theoretical underpinning. As cleaning a wound is more important than understanding microbiology, practicing compassion is more important than understanding quantum nonlocality.

It is the burden of only a few of us to understand the details of emptiness and its relationship to physics and universal compassion. Of course, as the Middle Way stresses, the deeper our understanding of emptiness, the more complete our practice of kindness becomes; conversely, to understand emptiness more deeply, we need to practice compassion more fully. Therefore, I fully acknowledge the synergy between emptiness and compassion but state the obvious point that practical expressions of kindness are more important than elegant intellectual formulations of emptiness.

Yet, there are innumerable ways to practice kindness. One appropriate way for some of us is to deepen the collaboration or partnership between the Middle Way and modern physics. If we can make the connections firm and clear enough, then as science inexorably spreads into every corner of the globe, its message of interconnectedness, of thoroughgoing emptiness, will also spread everywhere. If the connection between the Middle Way and modern physics is sufficiently strong, we will realize that this interdependence must express itself in universal compassion. For as the Middle Way makes clear, philosophic error, such as the belief in independent existence, generates suffering, while truth generates freedom from suffering.

It may seem unrealistically visionary, perhaps terminally naïve, to think that a wider appreciation of how nature is completely lacking in independent existence can encourage more compassion in our cruel world. Yet, the very emptiness of persons guarantees that we can change, we can improve, both as individuals and as groups. I also take some comfort in realizing just how young we are as a species from an astronomical point of view. Although there are debates about the exact age of our species, most experts claim it is approximately 200 thousand years old.[7] Others suggest about half this age. In either case, this is a blink of an eye from an astronomical perspective, where the relevant time scale is the 4.5 billion year age of the earth. To get a better sense of how young we are as a species, convert these numbers into lengths. Let 4.5 billion years scale to the height of a man (say, six feet); in this case, 200 thousand years would scale to approximately the diameter of one hair. Written language, which is 6,000 years old, would scale to 1/30 of a hair's diameter. I, therefore, have hope that our species still has much evolution ahead of it and that modern science and technology are helping speed it up. The speed and direction of our evolution as a species are debatable, but it does seem clear that, because of our warlike tendencies and our destruction of the environment, we are at a critical point. If we do not reconnect love and knowledge, do not appreciate that compassion and emptiness are the twin jewels of reality, then we are doomed as a species.

Because of the power of the technology bequeathed to us by science, we now have the ability to destroy our planet and ourselves. Several trends show that we are making rapid progress in that direction. Whether it is global warming, the proliferation of nuclear weapons, global terrorism, or the reality that "we all live downstream," our very survival as a species demands that we appreciate our profound interconnectedness. This deep interconnectedness, whether at the level of elementary quantum objects or the reality of global warming, inexorably forces us into cooperation and more concern for others. For example, Sweden has committed to be free of all fossil fuels by 2020.[8] Sweden is setting a superb example, yet if other nations do not cooperate and make similar commitments, little gets accomplished for the health of our planet and it inhabitants. This escalating global ecological crisis forces us to appreciate a very practical level of interconnectedness and the need for mutual concern for each other and succeeding generations. Therefore, from a simple Darwinian point of view, if we cannot reunite love and knowledge, kindness and understanding, then we are close to the end of our history.

Science can clearly be a force for great good or equally great destruction and evil. This is just as true of religion. Their collaboration can be of the greatest value, an enormous opportunity to take the next step in our evolution as a species. In the first chapter, I quoted the last paragraph of *The Universe in a Single Atom*, where the emanation of the Bodhisattva of Compassion, the Dalai Lama, tells us about the far-reaching potential of the science and Buddhism collaboration to meet the many pressing challenges to humanity. He concludes with, "We are all in this together. May each of us, as a member of the human family, respond to the moral obligation to make this collaboration possible. This is my heartfelt plea."[9]

The Dalai Lama is not given to overstatement or dramatic gestures. Why then does he speak about "moral obligation" and make such a direct and heartfelt plea? No doubt he appreciates that science will inexorably penetrate every corner of our globe. I propose that, if the collaboration is sufficiently developed, the message of universal compassion will ride along with the spread of science, and great progress will be made in fulfilling the bodhisattva vow—the highest moral obligation for a Mahayana Buddhist. His Holiness understands that, if the humanizing force of Buddhism is closely wed to science, we would see a great flowering of compassion, and this knowledge fuels his heartfelt plea. The Dalai Lama writes, "Perhaps the most important point is to ensure that science never becomes divorced from the basic human feeling of empathy with our fellow beings."[10]

The Middle Way teaches that empathically entering into the suffering all around us is a wide doorway to compassion. As I discussed in chapter 2, we can follow Shantideva and cultivate empathy through exchanging self for other. We can also open to the suffering surrounding us, whether unwittingly as in my experience in the Barcelona airport or more consciously by increasing our awareness of our "fellow beings" and the world in which we live. Although Naomi Shihab Nye does not have any obvious connection to Buddhism, her poem "Kindness," quoted below, clearly expresses this deep connection between suffering and compassion or, as she writes, sorrow and kindness. May each of us let in the suffering all around us and from it find our route to compassion, whether through the Buddhism–science collaboration or simple acts of concern for others and the world in which we live. Then, our compassionate action would truly express the interconnected universe revealed by modern physics, and we would give birth to a union of love and knowledge.

Before you know what kindness really is
you must lose things,
feel the future dissolve in a moment
like salt in a weakened broth.
What you held in your hand,
what you counted and carefully saved,
all this must go so you know
how desolate the landscape can be
between the regions of kindness.
How you ride and ride
thinking the bus will never stop,
the passengers eating maize and chicken
will stare out the window forever.
Before you learn the tender gravity of kindness,
you must travel where the Indian in a white poncho
lies dead by the side of the road.
You must see how this could be you,
how he too was someone
who journeyed through the night with plans
and the simple breath that kept him alive.
Before you know kindness as the deepest thing inside,
you must know sorrow as the other deepest thing.
You must wake up with sorrow.
You must speak to it till your voice
catches the thread of all sorrows
and you see the size of the cloth.
Then it is only kindness that makes sense anymore,
only kindness that ties your shoes
and sends you out into the day to mail letters and purchase bread,
only kindness that raises its head
from the crowd of the world to say
It is I you have been looking for,
and then goes with you everywhere
like a shadow or a friend.[11]

Notes

Chapter 1

1. Anton Zeilinger, "Encounters between Buddhist and Quantum Epistemologies" in *Buddhism and Science: Breaking New Ground*, ed. Alan Wallace (New York: Columbia University Press, 2003), 389.
2. The Dalai Lama, *The Universe in a Single Atom* (New York: Morgan Road Books, 2005), 209.
3. Victor Mansfield, *Synchronicity, Science, and Soul-Making: Understanding Jungian Synchronicity Through Physics, Buddhism, and Philosophy* (Chicago: Open Court Publications, 1995); *Head and Heart: A Personal Exploration of Science and the Sacred* (Chicago: Quest Books, 2002); including numerous interdisciplinary publications, such as V. N. Mansfield, "Madhyamika Buddhism and Quantum Mechanics: Beginning a Dialogue," *International Philosophical Quarterly* 29, no. 4 (1989): 371; "Relativity in Madhyamika Buddhism and Modern Physics," *Philosophy East and West* 40, no. 1 (1990): 59; "Possible Worlds, Quantum Mechanics, and Middle Way Buddhism," *Symposium on the Foundations of Modern Physics 1990* (Singapore: World Scientific Publishing, 1990), 242–60; "Tsongkhapa's Bell, Bell's Inequality, and Madhyamika Emptiness," *Tibet Journal* 15, no. 1 (1990): 42; "Counterfactuals, Quantum Mechanics, and Madhyamika Buddhism," *Anthology of the Fo Kuang Shan International Buddhist Conference* (Taiwan: R.O.C., 1990), 333–48; "Time in Madhyamika Buddhism and Modern Physics," *Pacific World Journal of the Institute of Buddhist Studies* 11–12 (1996): 10–27; "Time and Impermanence in Middle Way Buddhism and Modern Physics," in *Buddhism and Science: Breaking New Ground*, ed. Alan Wallace (New York: Columbia University Press, 2003), 305–21 ; "Tibetan Buddhism and Jungian Psychology," in *Buddhist Thought and Applied Psychological Research: Transcending Boundaries*, eds. D. K. Nauriyal, Michael S. Drummond, and Y. B. Lal (London: Routledge, 2006), 209–26 .
4. Ravi Ravindra, *Science and Spirit* (New York: Paragon House, 1991), 146.
5. Arthur Zajonc, ed. and narrator, *The New Physics and Cosmology: Dialogues with the Dalai Lama* (New York: Oxford University Press, 2004).
6. Alan Wallace, ed., *Buddhism and Science: Breaking New Ground* (New York: Columbia University Press, 2003).
7. Victor Mansfield, a review of *The Quantum and the Lotus: A Journey to the Frontiers Where Science and Buddhism Meet*, by M. Ricard and T. X. Thuan in *Theology and Science* 2, no. 1 (2004): 54.

8. D. K. Nauriyal, Michael S. Drummond, and Y. B. Lal, eds., *Buddhist Thought and Applied Psychological Research: Transcending Boundaries* (London: Routledge, 2006).
9. Richard Feynman, *The Feynman Lectures in Physics* (New York: Addison-Wesley Publications, 1989), 1:1.
10. The Dalai Lama, *Universe in a Single Atom*, 24.
11. Robert Thurman, *Tsong Khapa's Speech of Gold in the Essence of True Eloquence* (Princeton, NJ: Princeton University Press, 1984), 113–30.
12. From the interview of the Dalai Lama by John F. Avedon in *In Exile from the Land of the Snows* (New York: HarperPerennial, 1997), 393.
13. Thurman, *Tsong Khapa's Speech of Gold*, 113-30.
14. Galileo Galilei, *The Assayer (1623)*, translated in Stillman Drake, *Galileo* (Oxford: Oxford University Press, 1969), 70.
15. The Dalai Lama, *How to Practice: The Way to a Meaningful Life* (New York: Pocket Books, 2002), 128–29.
16. Juan Ramón Jiménez, "Oceans," trans. Robert Bly, in *The Soul Is Here for Its Own Joy* (New York: HarperCollins, 1995), 246.
17. Paul Reps, ed., *Zen Flesh Zen Bones* (Rutland, VT: Charles E. Tuttle, 1957), 56–57
18. The Dalai Lama, *The Meaning of Life* (London: Wisdom Books, 2000); *How to Practice: The Way to a Meaningful Life* (New York: Pocket Books, 2002).
19. http://www.tibet.com/DL/forum-2000.html.
20. Steven Weinberg, *The First Three Minutes* (New York: Basic Books, 1977), 131–32.
21. Steven Weinberg, *Dreams of a Final Theory* (New York: Vantage Books, 1993), 53. The italics are in the original.
22. The Dalai Lama, *Universe in a Single Atom*, 4.
23. Dilgo Khyentse, *The Wish-Fulfilling Jewel: The Practice of Guru Yoga according to the Longchen Nyingthig Tradition* (Boston: Shambhala, 1999), 3.
24. The Dalai Lama, *Ethics for the New Millennium* (New York: Riverhead Books, 1999), 123.
25. The Dalai Lama, *Universe in a Single Atom*, 2–3.
26. Ibid., 5.
27. Richard J. Davidson, Jon Kabat-Zinn, Jessica Schumacher et al.; "Patient Alterations in Brain and Immune Function Produced by Mindfulness Meditation," *Psychosomatic Medicine* 65, no. 4 (July–Aug. 2003): 564–70; Antoine Lutz, Lawrence L. Greischar, Nancy B. Rawlings et al., "Long-term Meditators Self-induce High-amplitude Gamma Synchrony during Mental Practice," *Proceedings of the National Academy of Sciences* 101, no.46 (Nov. 16, 2004): 16369–73; Sara W. Lazar et al., "Meditation Experience is Associated with Increased Cortical Thickness" in *Neuroreport* 16, no. 17 (Nov. 28, 2005):1893–97.
28. The Dalai Lama, *Universe in a Single Atom*, 10.
29. Weinberg, *Dreams of a Final Theory*, 168–69. Italics are in the original.
30. The Dalai Lama, *Universe in a Single Atom*, 208–9.

Chapter 2

1. Tenzin Gyatso the Dalai Lama, *The Compassionate Life* (London: Wisdom Publications, 2001), 21–22.
2. Shantideva, *A Guide to the Bodhisattva's Way of Life*, trans. Stephen Batchelor (Dharamsala, India: Library of Tibetan Works & Archives, 1979), 120.
3. Ibid., 119.
4. Ibid., 122.
5. Ibid., 123.
6. Ibid., 124.
7. Kelsang Gyatso, *Meaningful to Behold* (London: Tharpa Publications, 1986), 276.
8. *State of Food Insecurity in the World 2002.* Food and Agriculture Organization of the United Nations. http://www.fao.org/docrep/005/y7352e/y7352e00.htm.
9. http://www.cdc.gov/nchs/fastats/overwt.htm.
10. Peter Singer, "Famine, Affluence, and Morality," *Philosophy & Public Affairs* 1 (1972): 229–43; "The Drowning Child and the Expanding Circle," *New Internationalist* (April 1997) 28–30. These along with many other inspiring articles are available at www.PeterSingerLinks.com.
11. The Global Policy Forum Web site describes itself as "[a] non-profit, tax-exempt organization, with consultative status at the United Nations. Founded in 1993 by an international group of concerned citizens, GFP works with partners around the world to strengthen international law and create a more equitable and sustainable global society." Data for the graphic comes from the Organization for Economic Cooperation and Development and is posted at: http://globalpolicy.igc.org/socecon/develop/oda/tables/aidbydonor.htm.
12. The Global Policy Forum WebSite provides much data and analysis of ODA and related issues. The quotation was taken from the report found at http://globalpolicy.igc.org/socecon/develop/oda/2005/08stingysamaritans.htm.
13. Roger Cohen, "Growing Up and Getting Practical since Seattle," *New York Times*, September 24, 2000, sec. 4, 16.
14. Singer, "Famine, Affluence, and Morality," 230.
15. Ibid.
16. The Dalai Lama, *Ethics for a New Millennium* (New York: Riverhead Book, 1999), 177–78.

Chapter 3

1. The interested reader can find a significant treatments of emptiness in Jeffrey Hopkins, *Meditation on Emptiness* (London: Wisdom Publications, 1983); Jeffrey Hopkins, *Emptiness Yoga: The Middle Way Consequence School* (Ithaca, NY: Snow Lion Publications, 1987); and in Kelsang Gyatso, *Heart of Wisdom: A Commentary to the Heart Sutra* (London: Tharpa Publications, 1986). A more advanced presentation can be found in Daniel Cozort, *Unique Tenets of the Middle Way Consequence School* (Ithaca, NY: Snow Lion Publications, 1998).
2. Victor Mansfield, *Synchronicity, Science, and Soul-Making* (Chicago: Open Court Publications, 1995).
3. Kelsang Gyatso, *Meaningful to Behold* (London: Tharpa Publications, 1986), 122.

4. Lama Yeshe and Lama Zopa Rinpoche, *Wisdom Energy: Basic Buddhist Teachings* (London: Wisdom Publications, 1982), 50.
5. Lama Yeshe, "Searching for the Causes of Unhappiness," in Yeshe and Zopa Rinpoche, *Wisdom Energy*, 39–40.
6. Kensur Lekden, *Compassion in Tibetan Buddhism*, ed. and trans. Jeffrey Hopkins (Valois, NY: Gabriel/Snow Lion, 1980), 92.
7. The Dalai Lama, *A Policy of Kindness* (Ithaca, NY: Snow Lion Publications, 1990), 58.

Chapter 4

1. David Bohm, *Wholeness and the Implicate Order* (London: Routledge & Kegan Paul, 1983), xi.
2. J. S. Bell, "On the Einstein Podolosky Rosen Paradox," *Physics* 1, no. 195–200 (1964); Alain Aspect, Jean Dalibard, and Gérard Roger, "Experimental Test of Bell's Inequalities Using Time Varying Analyzers," *Physical Review Letters* 49, no. 1804–1807 (1982); W. Tittel, H. Brendel, J. Zbinden, and N. Gisin, "Violation of Bell Inequalities by Photons More Than 10 km Apart," *Physical Review Letters* 81 (1998): 3563–66; M. A. Rowe, D. Kielpinski, V. Meyer, C. A. Sackett, W. M. Itano, C. Monroe, and D. J. Wineland. "Experimental Violation of a Bell's Inequality with Efficient Detection," *Nature* 409 (2001): 791–94.
3. Albert Einstein, B. Podolsky, and N. Rosen, "Can Quantum-mechanical Descriptions of Physical Reality be Considered Complete?" *Physical Review* 47, no. 777–780 (1935).
4. John A. Wheeler and Wojciech H. Zurek (*Quantum Theory and Measurement* [Princeton, NJ: Princeton University Press, 1983]) give a detailed account of these debates along with reprints of all the key papers.
5. Niels Bohr, "Can Quantum-mechanical Description of Physical Reality Be Considered Complete?" *Physical Review* 48 (1935): 696–702.
6. L. Rosenfeld, "Niels Bohr in the Thirties: Consolidation and Extension of the Conception of Complementarity" reprinted in Wheeler and Zurek, *Quantum Theory and Measurement*, 142–43.
7. Bohr, "Can Quantum-mechanical Description," 699.
8. Niels Bohr, "Discussion with Einstein on Epistemological Problems in Atomic Physics," in P. A. Schilpp, *Albert Einstein: Philosopher–Scientist*, Library of Living Philosophers (Evanston, IL: Open Court Publishing, 1949), 218.
9. Abraham Pais, *Einstein Lived Here* (New York: Oxford University Press, 1994), 40.
10. Ibid., 41–42.
11. David Bohm, "A Suggested Interpretation of the Quantum Theory in Terms of 'Hidden' Variables, I and II," *Physical Review* 85, no. 166–193 (1952).
12. Bell, "On the Einstein Podolosky Rosen Paradox."
13. David Bohm, *Quantum Theory* (Englewood Cliffs, NJ: Prentice-Hall, 1951), chap. 22.
14. Victor Mansfield, *Synchronicity, Science, and Soul-Making* (Chicago: Open Court Publications, 1995).
15. Albert Einstein, "Einstein on Locality and Separability," (1949) trans. Donald Howard, *Studies in History and Philosophy of Science* 16, no. 3 (1985): 187–88.

16. V. Mansfield, "Madhyamika Buddhism and Modern Physics: Beginning a Dialogue," *International Philosophical Quarterly* 29 (1989): 371–92.
17. Aspect, Dalibard, and Roger, "Experimental Test of Bell's Inequalities."
18. Einstein, "Einstein on Locality and Separability," 186.
19. Bohr, "Discussion with Einstein," in Schilpp, *Albert Einstein*, 237–38.
20. Michael Battle, *Reconciliation: The Ubuntu Theology of Desmond Tutu* (Cleveland, OH: Pilgrim Press, 1997), 35.
21. Tenzin Gyatso the Dalai Lama, *Ancient Wisdom, Modern World: Ethics for the New Millennium* (London: Little, Brown and Company, 2001), 118.
22. Ibid., 28.

Chapter 5

1. Arthur Zajonc, *The New Physics and Cosmology: Dialogues with the Dalai Lama* (New York: Oxford University Press, 2004).
2. The Dalai Lama, *The Universe in a Single Atom: The Convergence of Science and Spirituality* (New York: Morgan Road Books, 2005), 112.
3. Alan Wallace, private communication, June 2006.
4. Richard Feynman, *The Feynman Lectures in Physics*, vol. 1 (New York: Addison-Wesley Publications, 1989), 1.
5. Geshe Thupten Kunkhen, private communication, August 2005.
6. D. E. Perdue, *Debate in Tibetan Buddhism* (Ithaca, NY: Snow Lion Publications, 1992), 544–49.
7. Daniel Cozort, *Unique Tenets of the Middle Way Consequence School* (Ithaca, NY: Snow Lion Publications, 1998).
8. Geshe Thupten Kunkhen, private communication, June 23, 2006.
9. E. J. Galvez, C. H. Holbrow, M. J. Pysher, J. W. Martin, N. Courtemanche, L. Heilig, and J. Spencer, "Interference with Correlated Photons: Five Quantum Mechanics Experiments for Undergraduates," *American Journal of Physics* 73, no. 2 (February 2005): 127–40.
10. Sidney Piburn, *A Policy of Kindness: An Anthology of Writings by and about the Dalai Lama* (Ithaca, NY: Snow Lion Publications, 1990), 28.
11. Harald Atmanspacher, "Quantum Approaches to Consciousness," *Stanford Encyclopedia of Philosophy* (Winter 2004 Edition), ed. Edward N. Zalta, http://plato.stanford.edu/archives/win2004/entries/qt-consciousness.
12. D. Adam, "Plan for Dalai Lama lecture angers neuroscientists," *The Guardian*, UK, July 27, 2005.
13. The full petition with its signatures can be found at http://www.petitiononline.com/sfn2005/petition.html.
14. Kelsang Gyatso, *Meaningful to Behold: A Commentary to Shantideva's Guide to the Bodhisattva's Way of Life* (London: Tharpa Publications, 1986), 29–30.
15. Image provided by C. Goldsmith, J. Katz, and S. Zaki of the U.S. Center for Disease Control.
16. Jeffery K. Taubenberger, Ann H. Reid, Raina M. Lourens, Ruixue Wang, Guozhong Jin, and Thomas G. Fanning, "Characterization of the 1918 Influenza Virus Polymerase Genes," *Nature* 437 (October 6, 2005): 889–93 (primary); *Nature* 437, (October 6, 2005): 794–95 (news). J. K. Taubenberger, D. M. Morens, "1918 Influenza: The Mother of All Pandemics," *Emerging Infectious Disease* [serial on

the Internet] 12, no. 1 (January 2006). Available from www.cdc.gov/ncidod/EID/vol12no01/05-0979.htm.

17. B. Alan Wallace, *The Taboo of Subjectivity: Toward a New Science of Consciousness* (New York: Oxford University Press, 2000).

Chapter 6

1. Jorge Luis Borges, "A New Refutation of Time," in *Labyrinths: Selected Stories and Other Writings*, eds. D. A. Yates and J. E. Irby (New York: New Directions Books, 1964), 234.
2. Victor Mansfield, *Head and Heart: A Personal Exploration of Science and the Sacred* (Chicago: Quest Books, 2002).
3. Eckhart Tolle, *The Power of Now: A Guide to Spiritual Enlightenment* (Novato, CA: New World Publishing, 1999).
4. In fact, the weak nuclear force is not time-reversible. However, we know that this time asymmetry plays no role in generating the arrow of time.
5. Victor Mansfield, "Time in Madhyamika Buddhism and Modern Physics," *The Pacific World Journal of the Institute of Buddhist Studies* 10–27 (1995–1996): 10.
6. P. C. W. Davies, "Stirring Up Trouble," in *Physical Origins of Time Asymmetry*, eds. J. J. Halliwell et al. (Cambridge: Cambridge University Press, 1994), 119–30.

Chapter 7

1. *Heart of Tibet: An Intimate Portrait of the 14th Dalai Lama*, directed by David Cherniack, 1992.
2. John Wheeler, "Law without Law," in *Quantum Theory and Measurement*, eds. J. Wheeler and W. Zurek (Princeton, N.J.: Princeton University Press, 1983).
3. http://hubblesite.org/newscenter/newsdesk/archive/releases/2006/23/image/a.
4. Wheeler, "Law without Law, 184–85.
5. Ibid., 194.
6. David Bohm, *Wholeness and the Implicate Order* (London: Routledge & Kegan Paul, 1983), xi.
7. http://www.archaeologyinfo.com/homosapiens.htm.
8. http://www.sweden.gov.se/sb/d/3212/a/51058.
9. The Dalai Lama, *The Universe in a Single Atom* (New York: Morgan Road Books, 2005), 209.
10. Ibid., 11.
11. Naomi Shihab Nye, "Kindness," in *Words under the Words* (Portland, OR: Eighth Mountain Press, 1995), 42–43.

Index